Overcome NOW

Audrey V. Hailstock

Published by Hadassah's Crown Publishing, LLC
634 NE Main St #1263
Simpsonville, SC 29681

ISBN: 979-8-9911882-0-3

Printed in the United States of America

Contents

To my awesome one and only husband,
Dr. James L. Hailstock and our
two outstanding children: Alex and Jessica.

To my amazing father and mother –
the late Rev. Fred L. Sweeney, Sr.
and the late Rev. Shirley Ann King Sweeney.

To everyone who came through and who will come through
the COMEFORTH ZONE.

Introduction

A new destination requires new direction. And though a journey of a thousand miles may begin with one step, that step should begin with planning, preparation, and purpose. Life is a journey that consists of many destinations that require moving out of the familiar into the unknown. Stepping out of your comfort zones is the biggest move you will ever make in your life. You see most people are moving, but not everyone is moving in the right direction. Have you ever felt like you were walking around in circles with no purpose, getting nowhere fast?

Life is more meaningful when following the right signs. I know most of us use a global positioning system (GPS), and we usually arrive at the exact place, at the precise time predicted. However, if the phone battery is dead or if there is no signal in the area, it's back to relying on the road signs along the way or asking others for directions.

You already know not everyone wants you to reach your destination. Some do everything they can to make sure you get lost along the way. Others simply have no clue and become the blind leading the blind. And then there are others who will help if you will listen. The purpose in writing this book is to help point you in the right direction. If you've gotten distracted and have taken a few detours on purpose, today is a good day to reset.

I have been in ministry for over thirty years, working with women of all ages and backgrounds. The hundreds of surveys (both formal and informal), conversations, workshops, and friendships over the years have revealed that we all need encouragement and guidance.

The number of broken, battered, and bewildered women who paint a pretty smile on their beat faces is almost innumerable. The complexity of what they've endured and keep hidden is unthinkable. Yet they keep on showing up for everyone else: the husband, the children, the extended family, the coworkers, and the church. Sometimes they feel lost, stuck, or not good enough. They feel overwhelmed and undervalued. The constant complaining, belittling themselves, blame, shame, and guilt cause them to remain stuck in an uncomfortable comfort zone. They've thrown in the towel. Have you ever felt that way?

Have you reduced yourself to living life on a hamster's wheel? The ups and downs and going round and round made you dizzy, delusional, and desperate. Yes, the divorce, the financial woes, the dead-end job, the unruly children, the trifling friends, the extra 30, 50, or 90 pounds, the rejection, the disappointments, mistreatment, being overlooked, being taken advantage of, the addiction, the sickness, the loss of loved ones, the betrayal by your bestie, the unanswered prayers, the abuse, the misuse, the depression, anger, the emptiness, the loneliness, the hurt, the pain, the shock, and the embarrassment have made you want to run away from it all.

It may not seem like it, but there is purpose in every step of your journey. The good, the bad, and the ugly. Sometimes it takes a while to exit life's round abouts. Don't become anxious when facing unpaved paths, roadblocks, wrecks, and speed traps. God has already made a way of escape. Trust Him. Help is on the way.

So come on, overcome now! It's not a matter of if you'll overcome, but when. I have the audacity to believe that with the right strategically placed signs, you are well on your way to victory.

You have what it takes to launch into your future. How do you do that? You take responsibility for the journey you're on. Yes, there are people around you to hold you accountable, but you're the driver of this vehicle. You're with you every mile of the way.

Overcome NOW! is written to uplift you and keep you out of the ditches of life. The signs, positivity pages, and Daily Actuation Plans (DAP) will enlighten you. These tools help strengthen what I call a healthy "habitational pull." Habitational pull deals with the productive habits you've developed that pull you in the direction in which you're going. Unlike a gravitational pull that pulls down, the habitational pull pulls you up and out. Focus on those habits that help you and don't hurt you.

It's time to stop reliving your past and start pre-living your future. How do you do that? Know your value and remember you are enough! Get ready to make the necessary changes in thoughts and behavior. Don't be moved by what others think about you. Be moved by what you know you are created to do.

- Unlocking the mind is the key to transformation.

- Transformation is what cranks and starts the action.
- Action is what accelerates manifestation.
- Manifestation is what steers you in the right direction.
- Direction gets you to the right destination.
- Destination is the place of celebration.

This is a personal journey. Doing the inside work is crucial if you truly want to overcome. Believe in yourself. "...The reality is that difficulties seldom defeat people; lack of faith in themselves usually does it."- John C. Maxwell

Commit this verse from Philippians 1:6 KJV to memory: "Being confident of this very thing, that he which hath begun a good work in you will perform it until the day of Jesus Christ." Have faith in God. But remember, "Faith without works is dead."

My word for this year is "catapult." A catapult is a ballistic device used to launch a projectile a great distance without the aid of a propellant. With your growing faith and words of wisdom, you will be catapulted out of your comfort zone straight into your COMEFORTH ZONE. I know you're ready to launch. You're not alone. Just promise that you will reach out to someone else and say, "Come on! Overcome now!" It's time to get into your COMEFORTH ZONE. Get yourself a sister, a friend, an auntie, a mom, or a cousin who will join you, hold you accountable, and watch all of you move to a place of power.

Let me explain the difference between a comfort zone and a COMEFORTH ZONE.

A comfort zone is a place or situation where one feels safe, in control, or at ease and without stress. This is where about 80% of people live. They enjoy just getting by, playing it safe, doing things the easy way, accepting regret, and being average. They take few risks, live in ease, and settle for mediocrity. It boils down to staying in the wrong zone. Don't settle for remaining ordinary. No matter how old or young you are, you can move from ordinary to extraordinary.

The COMEFORTH ZONE is an atmosphere in which you aspire to ignite your greatness in such a way that you impact, heal, change, inspire others within your reach. Yes, you may feel some comfort, but you don't allow it to paralyze you or keep you from accelerating, moving forward and upward.

The whole intention of this book is to inspire you to overcome obstacles and view them as opportunities and openings to the new and the next.

Part 1

A Mindset Reset

Chapter 1
Comfort Zone ~vs~ The Comeforth Zone

"I have said these things to you, that in me you may have peace. In the world you will have tribulation. But take heart; I have overcome the world." (John 16:33 KJV)

Overcoming is one of the best feelings in the world. We all have the desire to do it, but many don't tap into the power to get it done.

You do have what it takes to face obstacles, major setbacks, unexpected changes and get your victory. I have surveyed thousands of people to find out what's holding them back and keeping them from reaching their goals. Most blame someone else or some life situation. Some of the answers included: my husband was not supportive; my children took up most of my time; I did not have the money, education or opportunity; I'm too old now; I will just wait; I don't have the experience; no one will help me.

Your answers could be the same as theirs. However, all of that is about to turn around. Blaming does not change things for the better. You have the power to get out of those dead end situations. I believe you are ready to make that YOU-Turn and start your journey to overcoming now.

Life is a journey with lots of signs along the way. Sometimes we follow the wrong ones, ignore the right ones, try short-cuts, or speed in zones. We see the sign that reads Slow, Caution Speed Bumps Ahead, or STOP. Yet, we roll on through. Or even worse, we get stuck in places we should have left a long time ago. Sound familiar? If so, become your own cartographer. Knowing which signs to design and follow will ensure you navigate your way out of comfort zones and maneuver your way into your COMEFORTH ZONE.

Have you heard the quote, "Life begins at the end of your comfort zone"? My response to that statement is life is already lifeing no matter what zone you're in. The question becomes: Is it your best life?

If you're like me, you know there is a powerful purpose that you were created to fulfill. You just haven't done it yet. I know I haven't reached my full potential. If you have doubts about your worth, let me tell you now you are an amazing person. No matter what kind of path you've been on or you're currently on, here's your sign that YOU-turns are allowed.

Make that turn. "Never let success get to your head; never let failure get to your heart."
–Anonymous

You may have achieved some great things, and you may have failed many things. But now is the time to get out of those wrong zones of defeat and step into your custom made COMEFORTH ZONE now.

I say now because procrastination raises its lying voice and says, "Now is not the time." When you hear that, you need to make a decision - do I just sit here, procrastinate, and put my dreams and goals on the back burner, or do I stand up to procrastination and yell back, "I'm overcoming NOW."

You must realize you're having a conversation in your mind. Just you and your thoughts. Lao Tzu said, "The journey of a thousand miles begins with one step." I say that journey of fulfilling your purpose begins with one thought –

the right thought. To get to the right thought, you must pay close attention to the right 'mind signs.'

Mind signs, like road signs, help keep us from being a distracted driver. Distracted achievers miss turns, get lost, and run into dead ends. Following the right 'mind signs' will lead you to your destination. We must learn to read and heed the right signs to succeed.

You know how signs stand alongside the road. They can be quite interesting, entertaining, distracting, informative, and/or obsolete. The key is knowing which signs to heed.

THE CAVE EXPERIENCE

Choices. Decisions. Consequences. We have to make them, suffer with them, or face them.

A few years ago, the world almost stood still…held its breath as we waited, prayed, and hoped for the rescue of young boys and their coach in Thailand. You may recall the boys on the soccer team had planned to explore the Tham Luang Nang Non (the Great Cave of the Sleeping Lady) Cave after practice. These young boys were with an adult, their coach, someone older and wiser. They just wanted to experience a fun adventure. I'm sure they were intrigued with what they might find.

What should have been a fun and short daytime excursion turned into what felt like a never-ending nightmare.

Why? These boys and their coach overlooked or ignored the sign posted right at the mouth of the Tham Luang Cave. Yes, the warning sign was posted. The Thai Boars soccer team was trapped in a flooded cave for seventeen days following monsoonal flooding on June 23.

They stepped out of their comfort zone. But the lesson we can learn is to not ignore warning signs. We can get stranded if we don't accurately weigh the risks involved in our decisions. They would not have been stranded if they had made the right decision. When you step out of your comfort zone - the area of feeling safe and in control, you are stepping into a totally new zone.

This new zone may or may not be what you're expecting. It may be a zone of fear, learning, or growth as depicted on many graphs related to comfort zones.

I believe these adventurers skipped being fearful because they put their full trust in their coach – Ekapol "Ake" Chantawang. The players may have felt they would learn and perhaps grow from this experience.

What happens when you jump from comfort zone straight into a danger zone? Danger zones, panic, red or alarm zones denote risks, probabilities of harm, frustration, overwhelm, difficulty, and possibilities of loss or death. Ironically, the cave visit was to celebrate the birthday of Phiraphat Somphiangchai – one of the team members.

What was meant to be a fun excursion ended up being a dangerous and deadly experience. Royal Thai Navy SEAL, Saman Kunan, died of asphyxiation while helping with the rescue. A year later, another Thai Navy SEAL, Beirut Pakbara, died of a blood infection as a result of assisting with the operation. Lastly, Duangphet Phromthep, the team captain, died by suicide in February 2023 at age 17. In the midst of adventure and challenge, there may be consequences that are not planned. We can, however, learn from them. A reminder and strong admonition to you is to always look for the signs. The sign at the mouth of the cave advised against entering the caves during the monsoon season. The sign literally read:

DANGER!!

FROM JULY – NOVEMBER THE CAVE IS FLOODING SEASON

John Adsit, Education Consultant, in his article "Warning Signs at Tham Luang and Similar Caves: A Complex Issue" wrote, "The entrance to the Tham Luang cave did indeed have a prominent warning sign and the soccer team went past it when they entered. Most of the explored underwater caves in the world have strongly worded signs telling untrained divers to turn around. He went on to say, "The posted danger appears to be more of a lure than a deterrent."

If ever you find yourself trapped in the caves of life, reflect back to see if you missed some signs, overlooked the signs, or chose to ignore the signs. Did your decision affect you alone or were others impacted by what you did? What did you learn from the consequences? Sometimes, the risks are too high and you end up in the danger zone.

THE COMEFORTH ZONE

Your goal should be to assess your situation and strive to get into what I call the COMEFORTH ZONE. Many zones overlap one another. So yes, you want to get to the growth zone. To get there, use the skills you possess and tap into the resources available to you.

With the boys in the cave panicking, the coach called upon some strategies from when he was a monk. One was meditation. The coach was the very one who led them deeper into the cave while trying to avoid drowning. He had the key to what would sustain them as they dealt with not having light, food, or any of the everyday necessities for seventeen days.

The coach taught them how to meditate and this is what helped them to survive the most trying time of their young lives.

They were stuck in a place where they could not move forward nor backward. They were at a place facing a wall before them, water behind them, and darkness covering them like a weighted blanket. They had to be still. Sometimes the best decision is to be still.

In your life, you may be in a similar predicament, feeling there is no hope. You may feel trapped, hopeless, and defeated. You may even be facing death or the death of things in your life that you value. In those difficult moments, your thoughts are the mind signs that could lead you to safety or deeper into a dark, dank, dungeon of danger.

THE RESCUER

Look for the signs, other sources, or individuals that lead you to the COMEFORTH ZONE. Recognizing you're in the wrong zone will help get you to the right zone sooner. Often it takes someone I call the rescuer. These people are the more knowledgeable others, someone who has a better understanding or higher ability level than the learner in reference to the specific task, idea, or concept, such as a coach, teacher, pastor, parent, peer, or another person.

Lev Vygotsky calls this our Zone of Proximal Development. It describes the space between what we can do without assistance and what we cannot do even with assistance. But let me place a bold reminder right here. I can do all things through Christ which strengtheneth me. - Philippians 4:13 KJV

Don't ever under estimate the impact of including the power of God. Your faith matters. My husband, Dr. James L. Hailstock, preached a sermon once and told the congregation, faith is a data point. I don't care how dire the situation is; there is room for another miracle.

Use the tools within you. If you were brought up in the church, you were taught how to pray. So, pray. Ask God to forgive you for making bad decisions and behaving in immature ways. When you've gone in deeper than you can get out, God is right there. You can't go too far that God can't reach you.

The cave experience is not just what happened to the twelve boys on that soccer team. The cave can represent any critical and vulnerable event we go through in our lives. Leaders lead us, yet can still get lost. Peers pull us into problems. And sin, as said by R. Zaccharias, "Sin will take you farther than you want to go, keep you longer than you want to stay, and cost you more than you want to pay."

THE LAZARUS EFFECT

Don't be so anxious to get out of your comfort zone that you risk life and limb for a temporary thrill. When the urge for change hits you, aim for the COMEFORTH

ZONES, and be like Lazarus when he was called out of the cave/tomb he was in. Jesus simply called his name. One Bible Scholar said, "In the Greek Jesus's words don't actually say the common English interpretation of "Lazarus, come forth, but more literally means "'out here'" or "'I'm out here'" in the way of an implied instruction to exit the tomb and join him outside."

Lazarus' name means "God has helped." It's imperative you know and believe God is your help no matter where you are. He can revive every lifeless area and rid you of things trying to kill the purpose within you. Don't be afraid. Don't be scared. Don't fear.

Be advised, the number one factor that keeps most people stuck in the comfort zone is fear. Yes, the fear factor is real. But when you recognize it for what it is, you are well on your way to getting free of a fear-filled mindset.

CONSTRUCTION ZONE

- ✓ Identifying your comfort zones will enable you to make proper plans to exit them.
- ✓ Be careful about who you're willing to follow.
- ✓ Not every risk is worth it.
- ✓ C.A.V.E. = Critical and vulnerable environment
- ✓ Pray about your current situation.
- ✓ Be patient when it feels like help is not coming.
- ✓ A rescuer may come when you least expect.
- ✓ Lazarus means "God has helped."

DESTRUCTION ZONE

- ✓ Refuse to allow comfort to limit your potential.
- ✓ Don't allow the label society put on you to become the life you live.
- ✓ Stop operating with a fear-filled mindset.

INTRUCTION ZONE

- ✓ Train your brain.
- ✓ Survive and thrive.
- ✓ Look for the light in every dark situation.
- ✓ Come forth and bring somebody else with you.

POSITIVITY PAGE Date____________________

"Failure is success in progress." – Albert Einstein

As you reflect and write, include today's date and be specific in naming and describing your goals. Return to this page with updates of improvements, successes, and failures.

Write about the things that have caused you to remain stuck in your comfort zones.

____

____

____

____

____

Name areas in your life that you want to see significant change.

____

____

____

____

____

Describe your COMEFORTH ZONE(S). What steps will you take to get there?

DAILY ACTUATION PLAN (DAP)

1. Pray about your life and how you can change for the better. Write one line of your prayer.

2. Find a Bible verse or inspirational quote related to coming out of your comfort zones.

3. List two things you will do this week toward accomplishing your goals. DO THEM.

4. Name at least one person who will be your accountability person…not just a yes-person who will accept your lame excuses and let you slide. This person needs to really expect you to do what you say you're going to do. Now call and ask them to hold you accountable by asking you about your goal(s) weekly.

____

____

____

____

Design your MIND SIGN:

COMEFORTH
ZONE

Chapter 2
Fight Fear and Fortify Faith

"Fear thou not; for I am with thee: be not dismayed; for I am thy God: I will strengthen thee; yea, I will help thee yea, I will uphold thee with the right hand of my righteousness." (Isaiah 41:10 KJV)

Get ready for the fight of your life. It's not a fight with some force outside of yourself always. The biggest fight is the one within against a fear-filled mindset when facing challenges.

A fourteen-foot tiger shark and a thirteen-year-old girl in the ocean would seemingly be the formula for complete devastation, defeat, and possible death. Two decades ago, Bethany Hamilton was attacked by a shark while surfing at Tunnels Beach on the North Shore of Kauai. But it wasn't.

SURVIVE AND THRIVE

Number one, she survived, although she lost her left arm in the attack. Many times, when we face the devastation of any attack, we don't rejoice enough over the fact that we survived. Can you just celebrate the good news that you are a survivor? It reminds me of lyrics from a song by Destiny's Child entitled, "I'm a Survivor." The song inspires us to never give up.

Let these words play on repeat in your mind so that you never forget you survived. In addition to Bethany surviving after losing her left arm, she returned to professional surfing and wrote her autobiography *Soul Surfer: A True Story of Faith, Family, and Fighting to Get Back on the Board.*

It can be difficult to see how anything positive can come out of such a traumatic experience like this. But her example of overcoming the fear of the actual attack and the fear of being attacked again is nothing short of amazing.

This teenage girl returned to surfing less than one month after the incident. I couldn't do it. My fear of water will not let me go beyond the depth of two feet at the beach. To actually surf and not know what dangers lurk in the deep waters under that surfboard...not gonna happen. But what did happen while I read her story and watched her over the last few years is that I gleaned from her resilience. Her example of overcoming and coming back greater is pure inspiration. She had to stand on the word of God. "God is our refuge and strength, an ever-present help in trouble. Therefore, will not we fear, though the earth be removed, and though the mountains be carried into the midst of the sea, though the waters thereof roar and be troubled, though the mountains shake with the swelling thereof." (Psalm 46:1-3 KJV)

LIVE AND LEARN

Take note. She taught herself to surf with one arm. She returned to surfing 26 days after the attack on November 26. She was competing again by the following January.

We can only see her persevering and moving forward in the physical. But I believe that fight to get back on board was an inside fight. Yes, we could see the aftermath of healing physically and the return to the board. But something much deeper was taking place inwardly.

Her testimony leads me to believe that God was right there with her. Truly overcoming is about that walk of faith. We must fight the fear and fortify the faith.

F.I.G.H.T. = Faith In God Heals Thoroughly!

F.O.R.T.I. F.Y. = Forging Onward Renders Today's Intensely Focused You!

The way you fight and fortify is making sure your actuation headquarters is right. Your central command center is key to everything related to overcoming.

Fear has a way of messing with your mind. It's like a dark cloud hovering over you with the threat of a storm. You already know the storms of life can be devastating and debilitating. A fear storm will cause you to run into a comfort zone for shelter and stay there long after the storm has blown over.

I implore you to run into and take cover in your fortress of faith. This is what Bethany did. She placed high in many of the competitions after her attack, as well as finishing first, second, or third in several.

PRESS THROUGH THE PAIN

Remember if you can just press through the pain, there is greatness to gain. I know nobody wants anxiety and uncertainty, but inevitably you will experience these emotions when fighting fear and fortifying faith.

Dr. Oliver Page, a medical doctor and health content creator wrote, "The comfort zone is a behavioral state within which a person operates in an anxiety-neutral condition, using a limited set of behaviors to deliver a steady level of performance, usually without a sense of risk." Therefore, as you move out of the familiar, refusing to be trapped and limited by negative emotions, know that you are being strengthened by every act of faith. Dr. Page goes on to say, "This includes seeing yourself as inherently adaptable, reframing stress, and believing in your ability to endure fears and doubts."

I know this to be true. When I set out to make my dream come true of finishing this book and becoming a world-renowned speaker, fear and doubt have been chasing me incessantly. Now that I'm facing the vast ocean of opportunity, I feel I'm treading in deep and dangerous waters. Waves of uncertainty still crest and crash all around me. Things have been unclear at times while I try to see through and maneuver through the murkiness of life to find the treasure chest of my golden goals.

Have you ever felt petrified? Other people have probably told you what they see in you. You hear it. You feel it. You even believe it. But the wall of fear is blocking you from seeing and being it. Whatever it is, don't give up on it.

WALL OF FAITH

When my husband heard God say start a church and build a new edifice, he did that. There was a process. It didn't just happen overnight. There were many days, weeks, and months of prayer, persistence, and patience. Today, it is surviving and thriving. After holding worship, rehearsals, Vacation Bible School, Bible study, baptism, meetings, revivals, and weddings at many different locations, we were able to breakthrough to a groundbreaking moment for this God-given assignment - New Day Baptist Church of Spartanburg was born.

We are so thankful for the YMCA, Dr. Kirk Neely and Morningside Baptist Church, Bishop Dr. Charles J. J. Jackson and Cornerstone Baptist Church, as well as many other churches, restaurants, Marriott, and members who allowed us to hold rehearsals and meetings in their homes.

If you have ever endeavored to accomplish something, you have probably stood on these words: "Where there's a will, there's a way." Those words override worry and overcome fear. Almost twenty years later, New Day is still being used by God to bless Spartanburg, South Carolina. It can only be attributed to fighting fear and fortifying faith.

The truth of the scripture in James 2:17 KJV; "Even so faith, if it hath not works, is dead, being alone" reminds us that faith alone is merely a starting point. It boils down to these sets of threes:

Start. Continue. Finish.

Motivation. Concentration. Determination.

Conceive it. Believe it. Achieve it.

Visualize. Verbalize. Actualize.

Focus on these words daily. Do what it takes to accomplish your goals. Don't be distracted, deterred, or disillusioned. I am inspired by the beautiful WALL OF FAITH at the entrance of the vestibule of New Day Baptist Church. I don't know of any other church that has one. But when Dr. Hailstock announced that we would build a WALL OF FAITH with bricks bearing the names of the members and supporters of the church from its inception, everyone was elated. The wall stands as a solid sign of unity, determination, and love of God.

This was a beautiful visual of the fact that this church is only here by the grace of God and the many supporters He sent our way. Each brick represents strength on top of strength. It has not always been easy, but it's been a blessing.

What visuals do you have built in your mind relative to your goals? If there is a wall of fear, today is the day to bulldoze it down. If you don't, one wall will become another wall, and then another wall until you're trapped in a self-made cave of fear.

LEVELS OF FEAR

First, you need to know fear is not just being afraid of something. Fear is an unpleasant emotion caused by the belief that something is dangerous, painful, threatening, or difficult. There are levels and categories of fear. An article, "The Seven Levels of Fear" posted by Stephen Cocconi, lists the following levels:

1. Apprehension / Discomfort / Covert Hostility / Resentment
2. Denial /Ignorance /Rationalization / Pretense
3. Fright / Reaction / Violence / Threat
4. Retreat / Worry / Despair / Dread
5. Terror / Paranoia / Panic
6. Numbness / Trauma / Madness
7. Apathy / Resignation / Collapse

WHAT ABOUT THE FEAR OF POSITIVE THINGS

Have you ever heard of the Jonah Complex? It's when you have a fear of success or the fear of being your best. This complex makes you question if you are ready for and able to handle the changes that come with success. Sometimes we just don't want to pay the price of success. It's called "success phobia" or "achievemephobia."

"Fear is not the problem. How you react to it often is. If you know what to look for, you can deal with it head on!

Heal yourself first. Forewarned is Forearmed!" (From an article on Michael's Consortium)

WHAT ARE YOU FEARFUL OF?

We understand that there is a healthy fear that helps us make good decisions that can keep us safe when facing eminent danger. You can be fearful of what it takes to be successful. You can be fearful that you don't have what it takes to reach your goals. You can be fearful about what others think about what you do or what you don't do. And you can be fearful about what people are going to say concerning your goals – whether you reach them or not.

I was just like that. I didn't perceive it as fear though. I just wondered about these things and allowed the response to be inaction. That fear foe paralyzed me in many ways, inhibiting me from thinking positive thoughts, making plans, and daring to do what it would take to finish even things I had started. Fear of what people think about the way you look is another big hurdle to get over.

I remember several years ago how concerned I was about my natural hair reverting after I'd had it pressed and curled. When we first started New Day Baptist Church, we met in the YMCA in the gym for worship on Sundays. That was fine in the fall, winter and spring, but when the ninety-degree summertime temperatures showed up to join the church, I was sweating like I was in a sauna.

I was leading praise and worship. Pastor Hailstock had plans to eventually broadcast on TV long before the days of posting worship on Facebook. I wanted to look descent. But every Sunday, it was getting hotter and hotter. And every Sunday my hair was looking worse and worse.

So, I got an appointment with my beautician and did something different. When I mentioned it to my husband, he said, "You better not cut your hair." Well, I knew I wasn't going to do that… I just wanted a style that would last and be cute through the hot summer.

While the beautician put the chemical in my hair, I called my mom to tell her what I was doing. She said, "Whatever you do, don't get a Wave Nouveau." I could have gone down the drain at that very moment because I had just gotten … you guessed it… a Wave Nouveau.

On the way home, I was restyling my hair and strands were coming right out. When I walked into the house, my husband looked at me. "I thought you were going to get your hair done."

Needless to say, that was not what I needed to hear. I said, "It is done."

"I know you didn't pay for that."

That was not a good day. I looked a hot mess and felt even worse about my appearance. During the subsequent days and weeks, I saw more and more hair coming out when I combed my hair. I started saving the hair in a drawer because I could not believe how much hair had come out. It got so thin I had to have weave braided into my hair to cover the top of my head. I was so self-conscious about others being able to tell that it wasn't my real hair.

At the time, I was teaching seventh grade English, and dreaded going back to school with a different style. If you know anything about working with middle school students, you know that they notice every little thing, make comments, and even laugh at you.

Thankfully, not one of them said anything about my hair. By the end of December, I could wear my own hair again. It was short, but it was mine. I went into the new year with a new look and a brand-new outlook. I had learned my lessons.

First, to listen to my husband because he didn't want me to put chemicals in my hair. Second, I learned never to be overly concerned about what other people think of the way I look on the outside. My focus was turned to my inner growth and beauty, which come from a close relationship with God.

Yes, it's great to try to look nice and present yourself in the best way possible. But I learned the hard way that hair is not my focus. God receives my worship with or without a fresh "do" because He's looking on the inward and He is my audience of *One*.

After that experience, I never let it bother me if my hair reverted because of the vigorous praise and worship, preaching and singing. I was fine with it. I still have that wad of hair to remind me not to get caught up with what anybody else thinks about the way I look when I am worshipping, preaching, shouting, leaping, or dancing in the Spirit. I can truly say *no more fear*.

NOW WHAT IS FEAR DOING TO YOU?

There are many fear signs in your mind. They are capable of distracting you, setting you back years, decades or even a lifetime. This is why you must fight the negative effects of fear. If you look around at mediocre people, you will find that many have great potential. However, they, too, are afraid to venture out of their comfort zones. Fear-filled people complain rather than come up with solutions to fix things. They conform rather than contend. They cower rather than confront real issues. They accept defeat instead of adjusting their level of determination. They slow down and stop when they should speed up and continue moving forward. They sleep in when they should wake up. They give up and give out when they should get up and get out of the wrong zones. They lack the confidence they need to make the changes that are needed.

SCRIPTURE TO HELP FORTIFY YOUR FAITH

Nothing is more powerful in a believer's life than the power of God. We get infused with that power when we read, study, believe, and live the Word. You should always have scripture on the signs in your mind so that they lead you in the right direction.

"So do not throw away your confidence; it will be richly rewarded. You need to persevere so that when you have done the will of God, you will receive what he has promised." Hebrews 10:35-36 NIV

"For you created my inmost being; you knit me together in my mother's womb. I praise you because I am fearfully and wonderfully made; your works are wonderful; I know that full well."

Psalm 139:13-14 NIV

"Let us then approach God's throne of grace with confidence, so that we may receive mercy and find grace to help us in our time of need." Hebrews 4:16 NIV

"So we say with confidence, 'The Lord is my helper; I will not be afraid. What can mere mortals do to me?'"

Hebrews 13:6 NIV

"So do not fear, for I am with you; do not be dismayed, for I am your God. I will strengthen you and help you; I will uphold you with my righteous right hand."

Isaiah 41:10 NIV

"Have I not commanded you? Be strong and courageous. Do not be afraid; do not be discouraged, for the LORD your God will be with you wherever you go."

Joshua 1:9 NIV

"Though an army besiege me, my heart will not fear; though war break out against me, even then I will be confident."

Psalm 27:3 NIV

"I can do all this through him who gives me strength."

Philippians 4:13 NIV

"My message and my preaching were not with wise and persuasive words, but with a demonstration of the Spirit's power, so that your faith might not rest on human wisdom, but on God's power."

1 Corinthians 2:4-5 NIV

Be advised. "The only way to avoid criticism is to do nothing, say nothing, and be nothing." -Aristotle
Overcoming the fear of being criticized is a major accomplishment.

CONSTRUCTION ZONE

- ✓ Your biggest fight is the fight within.
- ✓ F.E.A.R = Face Everything and Rise. ~ah!
- ✓ A can-do mindset can get you through anything in life.
- ✓ You can.
- ✓ Learn that every lesson has a blessing.

DESTRUCTION ZONE

- ✓ Fear / reverence God in all you do.
- ✓ F.E.A.R. = Fulfill Every Assignment Regardless.
- ✓ F.O.R.T.I.F.Y. = Forging Onward Renders Today's Intensely Focused You!
- ✓ ~ah! = Actuation Headquarters ...Get your head in the game.

INSTRUCTION ZONE

- ✓ Stop worrying about other people's opinion of you.
- ✓ Don't be overly concern about what people think about your failures or successes.
- ✓ F.E.A.R = Forget Everything and Run.
- ✓ C.A.V.E. = Critical and Vulnerable Environment

POSITIVITY PAGE DATE ____________________

"The way to develop self-confidence is to do the thing you fear and get a record of successful experiences behind you." - William Jennings Bryan

Write about the things that you fear. Consider the things you are afraid to do but want to do.

____

____

____

____

____

Reflect on why you are fearful of these things or accomplishing something new.

____

____

____

____

____

Describe how your new focused you compares to the old you.

____

____

____

DAILY ACTUATION PLAN (DAP)

1. Pray about ways to fight fear and fortify your faith. Be silent. Now listen to what God is saying to you. Write what you believe God wants you to do.

2. Find a Bible verse or an inspirational quote related to overcoming fear or increasing faith.

3. List two things you will do this week in order to fight a fear you have. Do THEM.

4. Share with one person what you learned from this chapter.

Design your MIND SIGN:

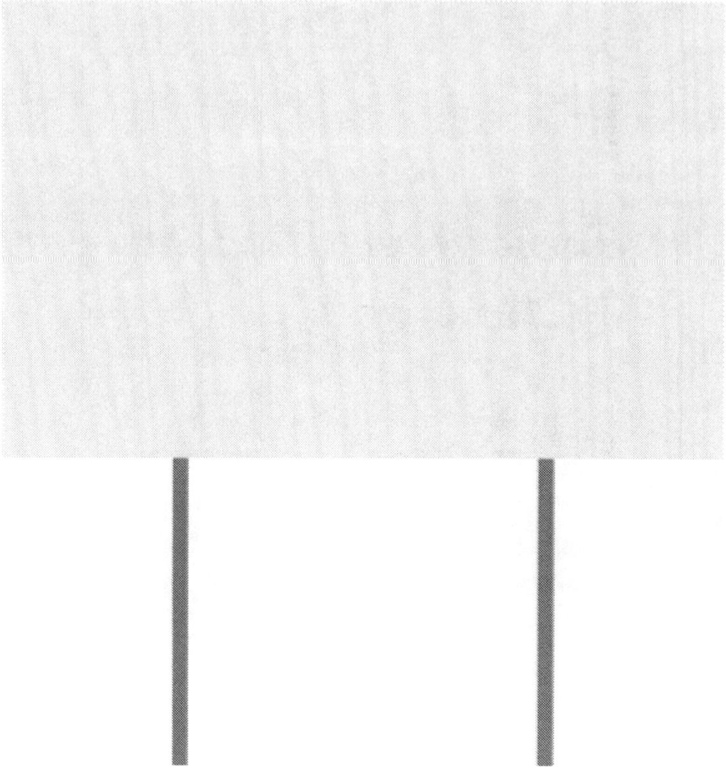

Chapter 3
Tame Your Thoughts and Manage Your Mind

"We would accomplish many more things if we didn't think of them as impossible." – Vince Lombardi, legendary NFL coach

An article in *Britannica* stated, "Lombardi imposed an unusually strenuous regimen on his players, most of whom had been accustomed to defeat." Now I'm not a huge football enthusiast, but even I remember the name Lombardi. In the same *Britannica* article, he was hailed the NFL coach who became a national symbol of single-minded determination to win. Clearly Lombardi was an inspiration to many because of his winning record. As head coach of the Green Bay Packers (1959-1967), he led them to win five NFL Championships in seven years. That included the first two Super Bowls.

We can learn something about developing a winning mindset from his example. Life is certainly more than a game, even though it's called the game of life. And yes, we should all be in it to win it. However, some of us think of ourselves as losers. I believe we feel that way because of previous defeats, negative feedback from others, comparing ourselves to someone else, and imposter syndrome. We give up the ball on downs by not keeping our head in the game and not giving it our best.

It's important not to miss the signs. Focus enough so you know when the coach is communicating the formations and plays. Coaches are essential when we get in a bad head space. They instruct us regarding tempo, plays and how to handle blitzes. Just focus on playing your position. Keep in mind, we can't always win, but we can always give our best.

No one is at the top of her game every time. You'll have times when you touchdown and other times when you fumble, stumble, and crumble. We all have days when we give up, give out, and give in. And that's because we're human.

CHECK YOUR RESPONSE

The strategy is to practice having the right response. No one should settle for mediocrity. We're always striving to excel. Develop the kind of mindset that is not swayed by who's around you or what is going on. Train your brain to focus and not be distracted by someone else's behavior, attitude, or rhetoric. They cause a bit of discomfort which is a good sign that something is on the verge of changing.

Signs you're ready to manage your new mindset:

- You're not as comfortable as you once were with certain ideas, outcomes, and/or people.
- You don't wait for the approval from others to make decisions.
- You're reading, researching, and reflecting more.
- You're cognizant of what you say because you understand there is power in your words.
- You practice positive daily routines.
- You press forward rather than focusing on the rear view.
- You develop a "no compromising on this" mentality.

WHAT HAPPENS WHEN GOD RESPONDS YES AND NO?

Inky Johnson, an American football player, asked this question when he lost his dream of continuing to play professional football, "What happens when God says yes and no?" Yes! NFL! NO…to longevity in the sport. You have to make up in your mind to overcome and not succumb. Inky said, "Tough times don't last…Tough people do."

He was preparing to play football in the NFL. In the second game, he was hit by an opponent and now his right hand and right arm are paralyzed. This led to Inkspiration, a ministry Inky uses to speak and inspire others. He understood that his life was not about himself. It was about being used by God. Even when he was living in a two-bedroom apartment with fourteen people, he knew God heard him. Although he faced all sorts of adversity, he kept his mind on God.

Overcoming obstacles in your mind is a mammoth feat. And let me tell you, this is a daily feat that some give up on. They are wrestling with the paradox of being blessed on the one hand, and literally paralyzed on the other. Same body. Same God. Different turn out. Different outcome.

Your mindset can make or break you. It's imperative that you don't let anyone or anything defile, deflate, or inflate your mind. In other words, don't allow anyone to sow weeds in the garden of your mind.

Your season of mindset change can be uncomfortable for others and cause discomfort for you. But that's okay. It's necessary. You're about to get the results you're working for – D.E.N.Y. Results = Doing Everything Necessary Yields results. In saying that, understand that you've got to keep priorities in the proper place.

Making a plan and not fulfilling it is worthless. I've worked with a lot of people and many students. I've found in the initial moments of planning and deciding what the goals are, they are hyped and the sky is the limit. When things settle down a bit, their level of excitement does too. And finally, when it's time to show the results, there are none.

I found this to be true when Sabrayla, a young lady I was counseling and mentoring, was going to save money. She had a specific goal in mind of purchasing a house and providing for her son. She started out great the first week or two. I would ask how did it go and at first it was, "Great, I saved the amount I planned to save."

Soon it was, "I didn't get to put my savings up this week. I'll double up next week." Next week came and she said, "I won't be able to save anything."

Then she avoided me.

People say actions speak louder than words. But I say results speak louder than actions. If you want something different, you must do something different. That difference comes from a growing and a maturing mindset that leads to better actions and reactions.

Don't be so relaxed in your stymied state that you can't figure your way out of the monotonous. You are not as comfortable as you used to be. You may not feel comfortable kicking it with your old circle of friends, participating in the same old routines, or doing what had become common place. When the mindset changes, it's apparent.

SHOW…DON'T JUST TELL

One day the butterfly and the caterpillar met for a visit. The caterpillar looked at the butterfly and said, "You've changed."

The butterfly retorted proudly, "We're supposed to."

This is the state of mind you want to have in life. Yes, I've changed. I had to. I can't just be the same when better is in me.

I remember when my son was beginning to eat healthier - "clean" meals. He exercised more. I didn't understand why he didn't want my good ol' soul food cooking. He wouldn't eat my homemade banana pudding from my mother's secret recipe. Before this change, he'd be right there in line to get a huge helping and come back for seconds.

He was conditioning his body so he could reach his personal goal of being physically fit. Of course, I didn't see anything wrong with consuming French fries several times a week, lots of pizza and pasta, butter-soaked Texas toast, decadent desserts, and lemonade with loads of sugar. After all, when life hands you lemons … you know what to do…make lemonade. I had no problem with these food habits.

But Alex sure did. And he had a remedy. He started cooking for himself. His daily routine was school, work, preparing dinner. His meal consisted of grilled chicken, steamed veggies with no butter or salt, a microwaved sweet potato without butter and sugar, and a container of water.

After a short while, everyone could see a difference. His body spoke volumes. Tony Robbins, motivational speaker and life coach, would often say he could look at you and tell what you are doing for your body. Because it shows. In most cases, we know what to do to improve. So, a changed mindset shows up in what you say, do, and produce. It starts with those thoughts that only you can tame.

My advice:

- Don't just think about it, be about it.

- Don't just say it, slay it.
- Don't just promise it, perform it.

Not only did Alex modify his eating habits, his exercise routine intensified. He improved his sleep habits, stopped watching television, started watching motivational videos, and started reading more books. His whole mindset shifted, and the results were amazing. No more average physique. He went from no pack to six pack.

Another major component for managing your mindset is having a definite 'why.' Alex recently shared that having a 'why' is imperative. The 'why' gives you a road map that leads you closer to your destination

This is excellent content for a mind sign. Sometimes it's just good to actually make a sign. Write the vision. I know people make vision boards. That didn't really help me. Mine ended up in a closet. What helps me get things done is having a clear and distinct 'why' and focusing on my daily action plans.

I used this strategy to finish this book. I have been talking about writing a book for twenty years. I've been thinking about it, dreaming about it, and preparing for it, no book. It wasn't that I was sitting idly by doing nothing. I was allowing everything and everyone to take priority over my goal. As soon as I stopped second guessing myself and putting my goals first, I got it done.

Every writing conference helped. Reading other books helped. However, the biggest help for getting over not feeling like I was ready or good enough was to stand on my own uniqueness.

In addition, it dawned on me the ladies in the COMEFORTH ZONE sessions would be even more inspired when I put my own words to work and reach goals that I've been talking about over the years. I was so busy trying to encourage them and push them to be the best version of themselves that I was not being the best version of myself. I had to overcome my own fears and doubts. And I did it. I can't wait to go to the first meeting after my book release. I will be that butterfly that changed. The answer to my why truly changed my life and awakened me to a more fulfilled life.

It's all in how you manage your mind. When you finally get to the point at which you want to reach your desired results – your personal goals in life, you will not be content doing business as usual. You feel like you woke up while others around you are still sleepwalking through life. You may try to go back to sleep, but you just can't get comfortable because the alarm has gone off. No more hitting the snooze button here. Come on. Rise and shine. You've hit the COMEFORTH ZONE. Insert your name in the blank. I, ______________________________, come forth with a new mindset!

Today's date: ___________________________________.

Now, did I take it personally when my son wouldn't eat what I had cooked for the rest of the family? No, not really. I just had to wrap my mind around the fact that this was the same son who used to eat my cooking, but now he's got a whole new menu of his own. Remember, we can't eat from everyone else's table when our menu has changed. Stop being uncomfortable trying to make everyone else comfortable. Don't be intimidated when you have to stand alone. Alex was the only person in the house eating clean.

Be okay walking solo on this stint of your journey. Your 'alone zone' will lead you to personal growth. Instead of feeling like you're by yourself, feel empowered to do your own self-care. You establish behaviors for your holistic well-being, leading to better health. Prioritize you.

Part of my preparation for this book was to select beta readers. I often have the participants in my COMEFORTH ZONE meetings read portions of my book and give feedback. I loved hearing their thoughts and reading their answers on the surveys. In addition, the main purpose of the meetings was to mentor them by holding group sessions geared to moving them from any wrong zones:

comfort zone, semicomfort zone, noncomfort zone, recomfort zone, or discomfort zone to a place to come forth. Basically, the objective was and is to inspire, motivate, activate, and cultivate them so much that they will move from any wrong zone into the COMEFORTH ZONE.

I would hold monthly sessions at Christian Supply, New Day Baptist Church, the Spartanburg County Library, Spartanburg County Foundation Robert Hett Chapman III Center for Philanthropy, and at the YMCA. One of my favorite sessions was held at the YMCA and focused on physical fitness. I invited my son to zoom in from Los Angeles, California to inspire the ladies. He imparted so much. One powerful nugget was this: "Growth and pain are the same."

But the most valuable gem was: "The bridge between where we are today and where we want to be is courage. That's the bridge. That's it. It's not somebody giving you a handout. It's saying, 'I have the courage to take the first step each and every day.'"

What I heard and what I want you to hear is that we must have courage… and that is an inside, individual, and independent job that only you can do. The way you qualify for that job is to invest in whatever it takes to ignite the spark that can light up any cave of complacency.

THE THOUGHTS THAT TRICK, TRAP, AND TRIP YOU

You must be careful about the thoughts you allow to linger in your mind. You could ask yourself, is it a trick or treat? Are these thoughts about to trap me or trip me? It's important to tame thoughts. One of the definitions of "tame" is to overcome the wildness of.

By the time Tererai Trent was eighteen years old, she already had four children. She was a child bride married to an abusive man. He did not want her to learn to read and said she was worthless. But she still had dreams. As part of her culture, her mother said write down your dreams and bury them deep in the earth. It took her eight years to achieve her GED. She said it was eight years of failing. She never gave up on her dream to graduate from college with a master's and a Ph.D.

Thankfully, she did not give up on her dreams. One particular word that she thought about from her culture was *tinogona* which means, "It is achievable." This became her motto. Her dreams were not hindered by the derogatory thoughts her husband planted in her mind. Rather she thought more about the dreams she had buried. She believed that whatever is ingrained in your thoughts can be manifested.

She achieved her dreams also by remembering that her mother would say, "Your dreams should be tied to the betterment and greater good of your community." So not only did she move to the United States from Zimbabwe, get her undergraduate degree and graduate degree, but she earned a Ph.D. in Interdisciplinary Evaluation.

Even though she was far from her land of birth, her mother, and the buried can that contained her dreams, she believed and achieved.

THOUGHTS DO MATTER

"Thoughts, whether positive or negative, emit energy. The energy produced by thoughts has the ability to strengthen or weaken physical health. As such, it's imperative that people learn various means by which they can take control of their thoughts. When people are in charge of their thoughts, they are in charge of their life." – Bruce Lipton *The Biology of Belief* by Bruce Lipton

Have you ever noticed how powerful your own thoughts are? I have. I recognize that some of the thoughts are interpretations of what we experience. We fabricate thoughts around what we have seen. When people say the biggest enemy a person has is the one within, I believe that enemy is a compilation of thoughts. Sometimes, the thoughts we have about a situation, person, or thing can run wild.

I've counseled many people who allowed their own concocted ideas about things to ruin relationships. Imagine a mother and daughter allowing a simple misunderstanding to rip them. The estranged relationship not only affected the two women, but the grandchildren as well. When they finally sat together to talk about it, each found out what they thought was not the case. It was a complete misunderstanding.

Wrong thoughts derail us and cause us to get lost in the wrong zones and stay too long. Here is where good communication can help tame your thoughts. The number of relationships that are impacted by wrong thoughts running around is astounding.

People respond by the thoughts they have formulated within. Even when you're challenging yourself to improve, you may think limiting thoughts, such as, I'm not qualified for this new position that's open. Or, I don't have time to learn a new language. Sometimes it's not other people who stop us from moving forward. It's us. We sabotage our own opportunities.

I almost missed out on a wonderful opportunity because I didn't want to take the test. When I finally decided to prepare for it and take it, I still had doubts. Talk about being nervous on the morning of the test. The outside may have looked calm as a cucumber, but the inside felt like a category five hurricane. By the time I took the test, I tried to lock in and focus. When I finished, I started thinking those 'what if' thoughts. The six-week time span waiting for the results felt like six years. I knew if I didn't pass, I would miss an amazing opportunity.

The walk to the end of my driveway to check the mail seemed a mile long. It was in there. I walked back to open the door to go in the house, and I was trembling with anticipation. I was about to fall out until I opened the envelope and saw that I passed the Praxis! If I could have tamed my thoughts and gotten rid of all the negativity and doubt, I may not have been on edge as much. I wouldn't have been bound by the fear of failure. I probably would have done even better if I had more positive thoughts.

Practice this when you need to tame your thoughts:

- Don't believe that what happened in the past is going to be repeated. So, what if you failed before, or gained the weight back last time, or lost the job.

  THINK: This could work out better than ever before, especially when I prepare.

  THINK: Even if it doesn't work out, I can try again.

  THINK: Other opportunities are available.

Remember: "The secret of living a life of excellence is merely a matter of thinking thoughts of excellence. Really, it's a matter of programming our minds with the kind of information that will set us free." -Chuck Swindoll

Be advised: "Successful people are not successful because they work extremely hard or have lucky breaks. They are successful because they think successful thoughts over and over and over again."

CONSTRUCTION

- ✓ D.E.N.Y. Results = Doing everything necessary yields results.
- ✓ Results speak louder than words.
- ✓ Allow discomfort to ignite positive change.

DESTRUCTION

- ✓ Don't allow anyone to sow weeds in the garden of your mind.
- ✓ Don't sit in sameness with people who refuse to change.
- ✓ Don't think like a loser.

INSTRUCTION

- ✓ Develop a plan for your own personal growth.
- ✓ Write those plans in a journal.
- ✓ Wake up and stop snoozing. Get up and stop losing.
- ✓ Don't eat from everyone else's table when your menu has changed.

POSITIVITY PAGE Date ____________________

Angela Duckworth shares in her book, *Grit*, that she was able to break away from the negative words from her father. Sometimes the thoughts you have come from negative words projected on you by other people. When you dwell on those words and put them on repeat in your mind, they impact you and may even hinder you in some ways.

Write about a time when someone spoke negative words about you, causing you to think less of yourself.

Write the opposite of what they said about you.

Even if what they said about you is true, it doesn't mean you need to keep those negative mind signs. It doesn't mean you can't change. Describe how you have since changed for the better.

DAILY ACTUATION PLAN (DAP)

1. Write what these verses mean to you as it relates to your thoughts.

   2 Corinthians 10:4-5 (For the weapons of our warfare are not carnal, but mighty through God to the pulling down of strong holds;)
   Casting down imaginations, and every high thing that exalteth itself against the knowledge of God, and bringing into captivity every thought to the obedience of Christ;

2. List and pray about one thing you need to focus on and accomplish. Date when done.

Chapter 4

Surviving the T.I.D.E. of Procrastination, Excuse, and Failure

"Be not conformed to this word: but be ye transformed by the renewing of your mind, that ye may prove what is that good, and acceptable, and perfect, will of God." (Romans 12:2 KJV)

A good reset is in order every day. Assess yourself often to see what needs to be built up and what needs to be torn down. We don't want to get into a mental funk.

THE PROGNOSIS OF PROCRASTINATION

P. Putting

R. Responsibilities

O. Off

C. Causing

R. Repeated

A. Anxiety

S. Stress

T. Tension

I. Irritation

N. Negativity

A. And

T. Toxic

E. Energy

THE EFFECTS

"Gallup surveyed 1,011 U.S. adults between January 2-22, 2024. The overall margin of error was four percentage points. Overall, 78% of Americans said they were either somewhat or very satisfied with their lives, a five-percentage point decrease from the 83% who said the same in 2023."

According to a 2017 article on Oxfordlearning.com entitled "Why Students Procrastinate," "Much of the time procrastination has very little to do with laziness or lack of caring. When you boil it down, procrastination is a combination of motivation, confidence, and comprehension issues." Other contributing factors listed were fear of failure, trouble concentrating, perfectionism, low energy levels, and poor organizational skills.

Are you living your best life? Honestly, can you say you are doing your best? Survey after survey seems to show that we are not living our best life. I watched a video in which Jim Rohn tells what the 98 percent (who are not reaching their goals) are not doing.

I believe that they want to do better but not bad enough to put the effort in to get out of stagnation. They are stuck in stagnation because they are attracted to and attached to procrastination. Although they choose to be there, they blame anything and anybody else for their current position in life.

I'm just as guilty as the rest. As soon as I share that I'm behind on finishing this book, I began telling folks all the things I had to do that kept me from being finished. I had to get ready for this sermon, that workshop, these Bible lessons, and another call. I had to cook. I have a thousand loads of clothes to wash, fold and deliver. I'm sleepy. I need to return emails, text messages, watch the news, and answer a long-winded auntie's phone call.

There are so many things we tell ourselves about procrastination. But here is the science behind procrastination as presented by John Rampton in his article, "The Science Behind Procrastination and How You'll Beat It: "Procrastination boils down to a battle between the limbic system and the prefrontal cortex. The limbic system is a set of brain structures containing the pleasure center, which the prefrontal cortex controls planning and decision making. Since the prefrontal cortex isn't as developed and thus weaker, so often the limbic system wins out, leading to procrastination."

My mistake or poor decision was to put everything else, basically the things I wanted to do, above what I should have been doing. You know what I mean. It's those valueless activities that I'd rather do during the time I should be doing what I'm supposed to be doing. My blaming other people does not get things done. It only puts me further behind.

I know this full well because I should have finished this book some time ago. But I had a million and one things on which to blame my behavior and explain why I was still not finished. You may feel the same way. But today, all of that is about to turn around. Blaming does not change your situation. You have the power to make things different when your actions line up with your goals. Inaction or incorrect actions both keep you bound and behind.

Now get ready to shake yourself loose, set yourself free, and move to the head of the line. If you have run into a wall of procrastination, here is what it takes to tear it down:

- Focus
- A plan
- Discipline
- Consistency
- Determination
- Drive
- Grit

Procrastination doesn't only keep you from doing some of the work; it keeps you from completing all of the work. Day after day, procrastination raises its lying voice and says, "Now is not the time." When you hear that, make a decision: do I procrastinate and put my dreams and goals on the back burner, or do I stand up to procrastination? The answer is, yell back, "*I'm over it! I'm about to beat defeat and overcome NOW*!

Remember these words form Edward Young's poem:

"The Complaint"

Be wise today, 'tis madness to defer;
Next day the fatal precedent will plead;
Thus on, till wisdom is pushed out of life:
Procrastination is the thief of time,
Year after year it steals, till all are fled,
And to the mercies of a moment leaves
The vast concerns of an eternal scene.

Procrastination is like a toxic disease we try to manage by ourselves. I've found at times we get a handle on it, but it lurks around every day to contaminate and infect the most productive minds.

If you don't want to procrastinate any more, here's the prescription. Read and do these steps every time you want to reach any of your goals.

1. Make a plan each evening for the following day. Write it down and include a completion time.
2. Don't allow distractions - even positive distractions - to interrupt your progress.
3. Ask for help with things you do not know how to accomplish.
4. Don't become discouraged when things don't go like you want them to go.
5. Regroup if you get behind on the schedule you originally outlined.

6. Don't negotiate with yourself when you should be handling something major.
7. Say NO! to other activities that don't line up with what you're trying to accomplish.

WHY PROCRASTINATON EXISTS

It's important to examine some of the reasons you procrastinate. Don't allow those reasons to become excuses that keep you stuck. Your objective is to realistically look at these and determine how you will overcome each one that's hindering your progress. Look at the list of reasons and place an **X** by the ones that apply to you.

_____ You don't want to do something that seems to be too difficult.

_____ You are avoiding something that you don't like.

_____ You have other things that you would rather do that are simpler and more fun.

_____ You feel as if you have more time than you really have.

_____ You allow distraction to be the main attraction. Even good distractions can be harmful.

_____ You focus more on the past and present, failing to activate the plan for the future.

_____ You feel overwhelmed by the project, the assignment, the goal.

_____ You are treading new territory with uncertainty (looking through lenses of fear).

_____ You don't feel qualified.

_____ You lack support from family, peers, or coworkers.

_____ You waste too much time comparing yourself to others.

_____ The timing is not right.

_____ Your priorities are in the wrong order.

_____ You are busy helping other people reach their goals.

Oh, my goodness. I need an **X** stamp. Looks like all of these apply to me. Procrastination is a difficult force to deal with. It has had a hold on me. And I know I'm not alone. Many of us don't realize the power in not using time wisely, thinking positive thoughts, and staying on task. The solution is investing your time thinking powerful thoughts that lead to tackling the tasks at hand. This poem by Edgar Albert Guest sums it up.

"Tomorrow"

He was going to be all that a mortal should be
   Tomorrow.
No one should be kinder or braver than he
   Tomorrow.
A friend who was troubled and weary he knew,
Who'd be glad of a lift and who needed it, too;
On him he would call and see what he could do

Tomorrow.

Each morning he stacked up the letters he'd write
Tomorrow.
And thought of the folks he would fill with delight
Tomorrow.
It was too bad, indeed, he was busy today,
And hadn't a minute to stop on his way;
More time he would have to give others, he'd say
Tomorrow.

The greatest of workers this man would have been
Tomorrow.
The world would have known him, had he ever seen
Tomorrow.
But the fact is he died and he faded from view,
And all that he left here when living was through
Was a mountain of things he intended to do
Tomorrow.

FROM PROCRASTINATION TO FAILURE

I sure didn't want to tell this to anyone. But I found out it blessed others, and it made me an overcomer. I failed my first semester math course in college. I was so hurt. I'd never failed a class before. It was a nightmare. I wanted to wake up and find it was the beginning of the semester rather than the end. But it did not happen that way. Instead, I woke up and cried some more. Needless to say, it wasn't the end of the world. So, tear down your negative thoughts about failing. All I had to do was retake the class the next semester. I did and passed. Hallelujah.

Of course, no one wants to fail, but if we do fail, fail forward. So that when you fail, you will already be moving in the right direction. In a recent article by Jennifer DiGennaro MA, LLPC, a psychotherapist and couples' counselor, said, "If you fail, that means you are alive and you tried. That is worthy of celebration." She also shared the following:

The 5 Secret Benefits of Failure

1. Yearning
2. Humility
3. Tenderness
4. Power
5. Vulnerability

"We delight in the beauty of the butterfly, but rarely admit the changes it has gone through to achieve that beauty." Maya Angelou

EXCUSES! EXCUSES! EXCUSES!

"Excuses are bad habits in disguise." -Anonymous

Excuses never change things for the better, but they do change things for the worse. So, give your excuses an expiration date, and let that date be today's date. Some of you treat your excuses like you treat your "exes." We get rid of them, let them go, say goodbye, for a moment. But whenever it's convenient, you let that sorry excuse back in only to find out, it didn't work the first time, and it's not working this time. There are no good uses for excuses.

The thing about excuses is that they sound good. They seem to make sense when you're faced with the 'whys' of life. They let us off the hook and many times cast the blame on other things and other people. They keep us walking around in a circle or even worse walking backward. If we continue to mistakenly view excuses as a soft place to land, we will remain in the quicksand of complacency. I've been there, done that and in some cases, I'm still there. However, at this point I am getting away from making excuses. For one thing, excuses led to bad examples for those following me.

One clear example of making excuses is when I used to be late for Sunday School many years ago. I just didn't like the way it opened up. So, I just made up my mind to come late and miss that part. Then when I started teaching a class, I couldn't tell my students to be on time and I was habitually late. I had to mature beyond having things my way and do the right thing. Now, years later, I'm early. I think of it this way - early is the new on time.

Some people may feel there is nothing wrong with being fashionably late. However, it speaks volumes about you and shows you don't respect and value other's time. Listen, if you are late all the time to everything, you have a problem. You can just go on and keep your excuses because we already know most likely they're lies.

The way to overcome being late and having to run in with excuses all the time is to get rid of obstacles that could slow you down. Here's a general checklist for getting things together days before or at least the night before:

- Is there plenty of gas in the car?
- Are clothes selected, ironed and ready to wear?
- Are my accessories together?
- Are shoes paired?
- Are my books, computer, notes by the door?
- Did I roll, wrap, braid my hair or pick out the wig I want to wear?
- Did I set the alarm early enough to get up and prepare breakfast?
- Do I have a backup alarm in case I accidently turn off the alarm?
- For those with babies and small children - did I prepare their clothes?
- Is the baby bag packed with extra clothes, pampers, wipes, pacifiers, powders, teething rings, bottles of baby food, spoons, burping pads, blankets, jackets, and toys?

These things could not be handled the morning of, especially for those who are prone to utilizing the snooze button and oversleeping.

These are things my husband would hold me responsible for since I was a stay-at-home mom. If you are a single mom or the one taking care of the babies and children, get over having to do it by yourself and just do it. Set a better example. Be prepared so that you don't have to get up every morning fussing, cussing, and hollering at everybody in the house including the dogs, cats, hamsters, and goldfish. Stop making excuses. Susan Weinschenk, Ph.D. said, "Making excuses is a bad habit. The good news is habits are changed one decision at a time." Make a decision to stop making excuses.

I'm convinced that people do pretty much what they want to do. When they say they're going to show up and then don't, that's telling. We all understand that emergencies happen, traffic gets thick, unexpected obligations pop up. But not all the time. Sometimes, people just need to stop lying. Just be honest with yourself and others.

The way to overcome excuse making is to not commit to doing something half-heartedly. When you give your word as a believer, keep it. "And whatever you do, whether in word or deed, do it all in the name of the Lord Jesus, giving thanks to God the Father through him."

Colossians 3:17. This level of commitment was so important that it is written about again in the same chapter. Colossians 3:23-24 says, "Whatever you do, work at it with all your heart, as working for the Lord, not for human masters, since you know that you will receive an inheritance from the Lord as a reward. It is the Lord Christ you are serving."

Check your level of service and keep in mind you're not serving yourself. When we recognize God in His rightful place as Lord of lords, we realize that we represent Him. How do you think God would respond to your excuses if you told Him what you tell your spouse, children, boss, coworkers, members, neighbors, friends, and even yourself? You do know God knows the whole truth. He knows your intentions.

The topic of excuses truly comes to bare when you address what God expects of you and what He told you to do. I hear so many excuses when I speak with people about what their purpose in life is and what they feel and/or know God has called them to do. I have broached the questions many times in private conversations and even at the altar during worship.

Has God called you to do something? Has he called you to a ministry? Has he made it clear what your next move should be? Many hands would go up. The "amens" would be shouted. And tears would flow. Yes, God is speaking.

And then the follow-up question: Are you doing what God told you to do? Silence or maybe one or two affirmations. But most are being disobedient to God even if they said yes to the initial questions.

You yourself may have told God and others some of the same excuses because you're stuck in your comfort zone. You're still developing. You want to wait a little while longer. Somebody else can do it better. Let me just tell you, God can use anybody He chooses to use.

ARE YOU AN ANYBODY?

This is a story about four people
named Everybody, Somebody,
Anybody and Nobody. There
was an important job to be done
And Everybody was sure that
Somebody would do it. Anybody
could have done it, but Nobody
did it. Somebody got angry about
that, because it was Everybody's
job. Everybody thought Anybody
could do it, but Nobody realized
that Everybody wouldn't do it.
It ended up that Everybody
blamed Somebody when Nobody

did what anybody could have.
-Emily Dickinson

Does this sound like what happens in your family, on your job, in your church, or in a group you're a member of? Yes, of course. Did you see yourself in the story? Yes, of course.

I pray the next time God calls your name you'll answer with the right answer and not the excuses, lies, deflections. Get out of the wrong zones: lazy, complacent, stagnant, snooze, pitiful, do nothing, spectator, procrastination, doubting, weak, low self-esteem, pass-the-buck, mediocre, clueless, merely existing, sleep, blame, shame, imposter, guilt, anxiety, critical, complaint, disobedient zone.

Don't start feeling some kind of way because I'm calling things out that apply to you. Just say "ouch."
Some of these same things apply to me as well. I had to and have to get over it so I can beat defeat. You would be wise to do the same.

"Think not those faithful who praise all thy words and actions, but those who kindly reprove thy faults." – Socrates

Design your MIND SIGN:

Be advised: Someone once said, "The easiest thing to do is to dream. The hardest thing to do is to pursue that dream."

CONSTRUCTION

- ✓ "It" can be anything. And anything can be conquered.
- ✓ Inaction and incorrect action both keep you bound and behind.
- ✓ An excuse focuses on the past; a solution focuses on the present and future.
- ✓ Focus helps you finalize and finish.
- ✓ Failure is not final.
- ✓ Reasons become excuses when they are used to avoid responsibility. -Susan Weinschenk

DESTRUCTION

- ✓ Pommel procrastination.
- ✓ Stop putting things off.
- ✓ "There are no good uses for excuses." ~ah!
- ✓ Excuses are like brakes. When you apply them, they slow you down and often stop progress. ~ah!

INSTRUCTION

- ✓ Let your purpose defeat procrastination.
- ✓ You may feel like you work better under pressure, but try starting earlier on your next project.
- ✓ Use the compound effect... Do small things each day.
- ✓ Be consistent in your progress.
- ✓ Say no. Mean no. No explanation.
- ✓ Make the YOU Turn!
- ✓ Use failure to refine and re-find your focus.

POSITIVITY PAGE **Date** ________________________

"Never let success get to your head, nor let failure get to your heart. – Anonymous

"A surefire formula for failure is to concentrate on excuses rather than positive action."

What was the worst experience you dealt with as a result of procrastination?

____

____

____

____

____

Share a time when making up an excuse was beneficial. When is it okay for you to use excuses?

____

____

____

____

____

What have you failed at that you regret the most?

____

____

____

____

____

DAILY ACUATION PLAN (DAP)

1. Evaluate your willingness to make up excuses. Are you pleased with yourself? If yes, why? And don't give me any lame excuses. If no, what are you willing to change to get rid of your most common excuses?

   ____

   ____

   ____

   ____

   ____

2. Do you agree or disagree? Write agree or disagree in the blank to reflect your views.

- ➢ ____________________ Excuses deflect blame.
- ➢ ____________________ Excuses are unacceptable for leaders.
- ➢ ____________________ Excuses stunt your growth.
- ➢ ____________________ Excuses convince us that we could not have made better choices.

Part 2

An Aha Movement

Chapter 5
Leaving the Cocoon So Soon

"When I was a child, I spake as a child, I understood as a child, I thought as a child: but when I became a man, I put away childish things." (I Corinthians 13:11)

What happens when your cocoon becomes your tomb? I hate to put it like that, but some of us get so comfortable that we don't move to the next level of our development. A cocoon is a silky web spun around the larvae of many insects. It serves its purpose of protection for a given timespan. Caterpillars develop into beautiful butterflies.

What happens when you leave the cocoon too soon? Development is more important than you may realize. Don't rush the process. Sometimes the people closest to you pressure you into thinking you need to rush your development. Your time in the cocoon is essential. After all, people don't know what it takes for you to reach maturity for your next stage.

Sarah Greenman, in her blog on symbolism, states, "The cocoon encapsulates both visible outer transformations and private inner ones. There is also a deeper message that for life to change, we must also change ourselves."

THE POWER OF THE STRUGGLE

This is the story of a man watching a butterfly struggle to get out of a cocoon. The man cut open the cocoon and saw the butterfly had a swollen body and small wings. The butterfly spent the rest of its life crawling, unable to fly. Yes, the man had the best intentions, but didn't realize the cocoon provided the struggle and resistance needed to grow. The restriction was needed because it forced fluid from the body of the butterfly to its wings, enabling them to grow.

Although you are exiting your comfort zone (your cocoon), you will emerge into your growth zone.

Most people desire change, but are not considering what's entailed in the process. The metamorphosis from caterpillar into a butterfly occurs during the pupa stage. During this stage, the caterpillar's old body dies and a new body forms from imaginal cells inside the protective shell known as a chrysalis. This process is called holometabolism. It is the complete metamorphosis in insects.

THE METAMORPHOSIS

For those of us in the process of overcoming now, we go through a type of metamorphosis. It is our Aha Movement which follows our aha moment.

The aha moment is defined as a moment of sudden insight or discovery. It hits you like a ton of bricks. You see what you didn't see before. You understand what was incomprehensible before. It's clear now. The light bulb is on. It's the moment clarity took place.

THE AHA MOVEMENT

The Aha Movement releases you from the cocoon you've been developing in. The aha movement births you into your new. It takes energy, effort, and endurance. Your reset mindset has taken place and now it's time for the big move. It's magnified movement. Tony Robbins calls it massive action. It's when you no longer want to remain stuck.

You have matured enough, been through enough, and developed to the point at which a birthing must take place.

Transformation is inevitable at this point. No one is going to rescue you. This is an inside job. With the insect leaving the cocoon, some cut their way out from the inside. There are some secret fluids which soften the cocoon so the insect can exit.

ECLOSION

It's your time. You will emerge from that place of development and protection. Somehow you will know when it's the right time. Things will line up. You'll feel it from within.

Enough is enough is the type of attitude you might have. Almost a don't care what attitude, you're going to make it happen. The lightbulb will come on. The actions will speak louder than words. The results will be bountiful. When the blessings bless you and others, you'll know it's the right move.

PACE YOURSELF

One of the best stories of a metamorphosis I personally know of is the one about Mr. J. T. Pace. How could an elderly African American, illiterate man go from being locally unknown to being nationally well-known seemingly overnight? No, his claim to fame was not due to some notorious crime committed or winning millions from the lottery. Although being illiterate may have felt like being isolated behind prison bars, Mr. Pace was liberated in every way except in his ability to read. But where there is a will, there is a way.

What prompted him at the age of 65 to want to learn to read? After all, he had done well in life. He had a "why" "why" "why." Whenever you make big moves, it matters if you have a Why. Mr. Pace's Why was tied to his desire to read the Bible.

"For most of his life, Pace was caught in a web. And upon finding his way out, he seemed like the perfect man to show others the way to literacy. One of eight children born in Greenville County into a family of meager earnings, Pace had little education. 'We were poor people. None of the children ever finished school,' he said during an interview at his home in Mauldin. His most memorable day in the classroom was the day he decided to drop out." This excerpt from an article in *The Greenville News* is powerful inspiration that you should not let age be a hinderance to you making your next move.

"I stuttered, and the teacher tried to make me stand up and recite the ABC's. And I couldn't. I froze. I was afraid I was going to stutter. And she hit me across the back of my head and tried to make me say it. And I got angry, so I never went back."

Have you ever experienced a frozen moment like that? All eyes on you. This was a horrible public display of humility and hurt. That's enough to make you leave and not come back. I'm just thankful that not all teachers are like that one.

During his time serving in World War II, Mr. Pace relied on others to read the letters his mother sent. After returning home, he worked in construction and as a truck driver. When he drove across the country, he compensated for his lack of reading skills by depending on help from strangers. For years, Mr. Pace's greatest fear was that those who didn't know he couldn't read might someday discover his secret.

Mr. Pace was in a type of comfort zone because as he put it, "It seemed like I had just about everything, but there was one huge thing lacking in my life. I said to myself, 'I have just got to read the Bible.'"

Sometimes a need plus a desire will become the force that catapults you out of the trap of your comfort zone. One day, he landed in the admissions office of Bob Jones University, a religious educational institution. He asked the receptionist if they could teach him to read the Bible. She smiled and said, "Yes," and handed him an admissions form to fill out. He then explained he could not read and wanted to read one book – the Bible.

The woman sadly said, "No." Mr. Pace recalls going home and crying about his dilemma. But three weeks later, she called and told him about the Greenville Literacy Association. From that day in 1981, he made many strides on his path to literacy by attending two-hour classes each week for two years. He would read first-grade books, then go home and try to read the Bible. One day, he became so frustrated trying to understand a particular passage of scripture that he decided he would quit.

We've all felt that way. Quitting may seem like a good solution, but it's not the best solution. Don't Quit!!! Don't give up!!! Don't turn back!!! Next, he did what I suggest you do when you are in an uncomfortable and frustrating place. Get in the prayer zone! After a night of prayer in which he told God he didn't want to go on living if he couldn't read, he opened his worn black Bible the following morning and the words made sense.

He cried, but this time for joy. He was finally able to read a simplified version of the Bible. He had freed himself from the invisible bondage of not being able to read. His life was changed, and he was able to be a great example for others. He reached thousands of illiterate people, helping them to change.

Messages from Mr. Pace's life are still applicable and inspiring today. He said, "See, a person who can't read is not stupid; they just can't read." He also showed that a deficiency in one area does not keep you from reaching your COMEFORTH ZONE. He was a South Carolina Department of Corrections volunteer and a member of the Greenville Literacy Board of Directors. He won local acclaim in 1985 when he was featured in a United Way public service spot on television. This led to the national ad with PLUS. He later won many local, state, and national awards for outstanding public service. He became one of nine people chosen from a pool of 8,000 nominees as a winner of the prestigious National Jefferson Award for Outstanding Service.

His COMEFORTH ZONE experience led him to even more fame and an ABC news story on his struggle, as well as an appearance on the *Oprah Winfrey* television show. It doesn't end there. On July 4, 1987, Mr. Pace read the preamble to the U.S. Constitution during a ceremony in St. Louis celebrating the document's 200th birthday. Now that's how you go from unknown to nationally well-known all while making a positive difference and inspiring others.

FROM MARGINAL TO EXCEPTIONAL

The impact of making a big move for yourself can bless others. Mr. Pace got out of his comfort zone and gained what he needed and desired. Talk about a blessing. His big move from illiterate to literate opened doors for himself and many others. Please remember that your COMEFORTH ZONE is not just about you. Your influence, impact, and inspiration will lift others from being stuck in a marginalized zone to being free in an exceptional zone.

James Allen, the pioneer of the self-help movement, was clear that, "Just having thoughts is not enough. Thoughts are just the starting point. And if we don't harmonize our thoughts with the right actions, we will never accomplish what we are set to."

FIVE WHYS

From not even having a GED, being taken from parents and sent to foster care, to being homeless, having five children whose father died, to not wanting to live, to having all the odds stacked against her, this young single mother, Iesha Champ, became a champion. She said she didn't just overcome those obstacles, she destroyed them.

She had a dream of becoming a lawyer since she was seven years old, but she didn't have stable guidance, according to a December 12, 2020 article in *Black Enterprise.*

She was encouraged by her pastor, Louise Holman, to get her GED. Though she was hesitant initially, she made the big move. She got her GED, earned her associates and bachelors, and graduated from law school. She and her children lived through the struggles and the difficult times. They're all champions!

Iesha gives all praise to God and is standing on her faith all the way. If ever you feel stuck or like just giving up, think about what she did. She started right where she was and started doing the small things first. Don't try to jump ahead and skip steps. Don't be in a hurry. Pace yourself. Be consistent and disciplined. Don't listen to the wrong thoughts that may be posted in your mind…like "You'll be a failure just like your mom." Or "Look at all the mistakes you've made." Or "Just kill yourself." Or "You're worthless." Or "You'll never be good enough."

Instead, you can start your big move by designing mind signs to combat every negative thought you have and post them all over the place. Write whatever counters those negative thoughts. Here are a few examples. Write your name in the blank:

This is your own personal "I__________________AM" page.

I, Audrey Hailstock, **am** finishing this book and publishing it this year! Hallelujah!!!

I, _________________________, **am** an overcomer!

I, _________________________, **am** changing the trajectory of my life by making big moves.

I, _________________________, **am** worthy and more than enough!

I, _________________________, **am** loved by God.

I, _________________________, **am** healed, delivered, and set free!

I, _________________________, **am** beautiful.

I, _________________________, **am**

I, _________________________, **am** wealthy and healthy.

I, ___________________________,
am fearfully and wonderfully made.

I, ______________________________, **am** doing all things through Christ who strengthens me.

Now here is your own personal, **"I ____________________ AM NOT"** page.

I, Audrey Hailstock, **am not** a procrastinator!

I, __________________________, **am not** giving up on my dreams and goals.

I, _____________________________, **am not** defeated.

I, _____________________________, **am not** stupid, ugly, or lazy.

I, ____,
am not

Now all of those declarations and decrees are great. But actions speak louder than words. "Declaration is what you say, but actuation is what you do!" ~ah!

"Never get tired of doing your best. Get tired of being as slack as the rest!" ~ah!

CONSTRUCTION

- ✓ People may not understand your transformation.
- ✓ You can encourage others even as you move ahead.
- ✓ Struggle within is an essential part of your development.
- ✓ Our struggles give us strength.
- ✓ A steady pace can win the race.

DESTRUCTION

- ✓ Don't wait on everyone else.
- ✓ Don't rush the process.
- ✓ Don't remain frozen.
- ✓ Don't expect immediate gratification.

INSTRUCTION

- ✓ If others are not ready to move forward and you are, MOVE.
- ✓ Believe in yourself.
- ✓ Watch one. Do one. Teach one.
- ✓ Let the heat thaw you out. ~ah!
- ✓ Get defrosted not defeated!
- ✓ Kneel into the prayer zone.
- ✓ Increase your ability. Accept responsibility. Cherish accountability.

Design your MIND SIGN:

GOD'S GEM

POSITIVITY PAGE Date ____________________

"Whatever you do, don't wait around too long for things to change. New paths are made by walking, not waiting. Taking the next step is what gradually builds your confidence." -Marcandangel

What big moves will you make this week toward your goal?

____

____

____

____

____

Recall a time when you or someone you know prayed about something, and the prayer was answered. Now write a prayer that you need God to answer.

____

____

____

____

____

____

____

____

DAILY ACTUATION PLAN (DAP)

1. Find/order/check out a book on fasting and praying. Begin reading it. Write one new thing you learned.

2. List the reasons you have not lived out your dreams.

3. Name and reach out to at least one person who could be a mentor or advisor.

Chapter 6
Identifying Image Issues, Insecurities, and Inferiorities

"I know what they are thinking, but why should it matter as long as I can sing? It's not a beauty contest." – Susan Boyle

She dreamed a dream to become a professional singer and it came to be her reality. Susan Boyle had a disability and was made fun of when she was younger. She is grateful for her strong faith in God which is like a beacon to her. Prayer is important to her.

In her early years, she felt slower in school. Her escape from those difficult times of not being able to fit in and being made fun of was music. She was a loner. Depression was a part of her young adult life.

January 21, 2009, she auditioned on Britian's Got Talent. One of nine children, at 47, she dared to say out loud she wanted to be as famous as Elaine Paige. The judges and even the audience members thought she was delusional and unattractive.

Within seconds of beginning to sing on the show, she embodied the song she was singing ("I Dream a Dream"), and the entire audience was standing by the end. Despite the initial perception and impression of her, she mesmerized everyone. One fan said he thought Susan meant there was no time limit on our dreams. She had the fastest selling debut album in history.

Susan went from complete anonymity to complete global super stardom. Such an amazing example of overcoming image issues. But even after an outstanding experience and national recognition, she was still on a rollercoaster ride. With every sudden takeoff and sudden stop, the ups and the downs, each twist and turn, life still happened.

HOW YOU LOOK TO YOU MATTERS MOST

You see no matter how talented we are, we all have issues that we deal with. Mental issues. Social issues. Just issues. They all come together to form our self-image. In the article, "What Is Self-Image in Psychology?" on Positivepsychology.com, self-image is explained.

The three elements of a person's self-image are as follows:

1. The way a person perceives or thinks of himself or herself
2. The way a person interprets others' perceptions (or what he or she thinks others think) of himself or herself.
3. The way a person would like to be (his or her ideal self).

What I want you to grasp is that it is not about the packaging. Even if the outside world seeks to promote packaging, you need to remember even the best packages wear out, deteriorate, and erode over time.

Sure, do the best you can in taking care of yourself, sprucing up, slaying, but remember there will always be someone who looks better than you and worse than you in someone's eyes. But when you look in your mirror, you better tell yourself, "I look fly! I look good! I am attractive."

COMPARING IS THE THEIF OF ORIGINALITY

Comparing ourselves to others is something we all do as humans. It can be beneficial by helping us understand who we are, what we might be adept at, and what we can improve upon. Comparisons could cause us to learn from others, grow in new ways, and notice our own progress. For instance, if we see that someone is better at a task than us, we might be motivated to learn from them and do better in the future.

On the other hand, comparisons can also have negative effects. Feelings of inadequacy, low self-esteem, and a competitive mindset could be the result of comparing. When we compare ourselves to others who are worse off than us, we might feel better about ourselves, but this can become unhealthy. Comparing ourselves can also prevent us from really living in the moment and just celebrating others. We seem to have this fundamental need to evaluate ourselves, and the only way to do that is to compare ourselves *in reference to something else.*

Here is another look at what comparing can cause. Your comparison has the potential to artificially boost your ego. You begin thinking more highly of yourself than you ought. You will probably inwardly think you're better than someone else even if only temporarily. Also, you may uncover vulnerabilities that were hidden before. This could lead to your feeling less than, inadequate, resentment, anger, envy, and shame.

The comparison zone, just ain't what cha want.

Learn from Susan's highs. Overcoming everyday takes getting out of your comfort zone even if it hurts. There will be days when every note is the wrong note and the audience is booing you right off the stage. Just know that tomorrow is a new day filled with new possibilities and new opportunities.

NO MORE COPY CATS

What God created you to do and be is not going to be duplicated by anyone else. Your set of circumstances, trials, tribulations, ups and downs, ins and outs, stumbles and falls all help to compose the most beautiful sheet of music you can be.

So, what if you don't sound like anyone else? You sound good to God. Even if you have to make a joyful noise to the LORD by your lonesome, do that. And do your best. He is an audience of one. Get over your differences, handicapableness, over-the-topness, standoutedness, extraness, and YOUniqueness.

As I say, why be a counterfeit when an original is priceless? Why be a copy when the real deal is more valuable? Why imitate when you can initiate? Why reproduce when you can induce? I think you got your picture.

Let me just let you know. You were created to be you. Like my song goes, "Can't nobody beat you being you...... Boo! So do you...ooooo!"

Now just sachet your best self right over to the nearest mirror and tell yourself how much you love yourself...flaws and all. Imperfections. Scars. Spots. Grays. Thinning. Hippiness. Big backness. Flat chestedness. Big belliedness. Skinniness. Thickness. Pal skinnedness. Dark skinnedness. Shortness. Tallness. Awkwardness. Simpleness. Ugliness. Prettiness. Trifflingness. Fearfulness. Braveness. Loudness. Quietness. Creativeness. Dullness. Averageness. And any other NESS!!! Just fill in the blank with you -ness

__________________________________.

Susan Boyle was considered an average Joe with a lucky break and lots of bad times. People laughed at her, but who's laughing now?

You may not have a story ending like hers, but God knows the plans He has for you ... plans to prosper you and not harm you, plans to give you hope and a future (Jeremiah 29:11). Relish in the Word of God that all things are indeed working for your good. It may not always look like it or feel like it. You may have to mourn and cry and endure hardness as a good soldier. You may not get the answers to every prayer in the way you want it or when you want it. But keep the faith.

You were made in the image of God according to Genesis 1:26-27. Whatever issues you face, you have access to the creator through prayer and faith.

INSECURITY ISSUES

An abandoned baby thrown in a dumpster like a load of worthless trash grows up to be an amazing boy loaded with a wealth of technical talent. His birth mother discarded him two days after his birth. An older couple, Nathan and Betty Mae Figgers, adopted him. Although he still faced difficulties, his life was on the way up from there. At nine, he got a broken computer and was able to fix it himself. At twelve, he had a job working with computers. He owned a computer company at fifteen. He also invented a special pair of shoes with a GPS tracker and a two-way communicator for his father who was dealing with Alzheimer's Disease. As a young man, he remained focused on his goals despite his tragic beginnings.

Working with computers took away the pain of being bullied. He couldn't wait to get home from school, where they would call him "Trash Can Boy" and laugh at how elderly his parents were. Grateful that his parents adopted him, he was still inquisitive about his birth mom because of the taunting from classmates who called him "Dumpster

Baby." The bullies would say, "Nobody wants you. You're dirty." He felt unwanted.

If you've ever been bullied, berated, or belittled in any way at any age, you can relate to how Freddie felt at such a young age having to go through this kind of treatment. The good news is he never let it stop him. In addition to owning a successful computer company, he sold his shoe tracker invention for $2.2 million dollars. He also built a smart glucometer that instantly shares a person's blood sugar level with their closest relative and adds the reading to their electronic health record for their doctor to see. This CEO now runs a $62 million dollar company. His birth mother, for whatever reason(s), did not know the value and treasure of the one she birthed.

I don't know what all has made you feel a bit insecure on your journey, but I'm sure something has. Insecurities can cause uncertainty or anxiety about oneself and a lack of confidence.

The average American feels insecure five times a day, as reported in a recent survey conducted by OnePoll for CURAD. Of the 2,000 participants surveyed, 40% were insecure when confronted with speaking in front of a large crowd, 34% were nervous when not properly prepared, and 28% were uneasy when starting a new job.

So, trust and believe, you are not alone if you feel insecure. Peers, parents, and people period have a way of tearing you down and making you feel some kind of way. It's up to you to get over it! In that same survey, almost half of the participants came to the realization that they needed to develop a positive mindset. In addition, being prepared, working out, and helping others made a great difference in not feeling insecure.

But over half of the participants stated that faking confidence actually helped boost their real confidence. In other words, "fake it 'til you make it!" In my words, "FAITH it until you make it." Put your faith on it. Secure your situation with believing that God can get you through what you can't get you through. Hebrews 10:35-36 says, "So do not throw away your confidence; it will be richly rewarded. You need to persevere so that when you have done the will of God, you will receive what he has promised."

Come on! Persevere! I know how it feels to be bullied, laughed at and mistreated. I know what it's like when people seemingly dislike you for no reason at all. The only title of a sermon I recall my pastor (Rev. Joe Stevens of the Mt. Pleasant Baptist Church on the White Horse Road in Greenville, SC) preaching when I was growing up was "Picked Out to Be Picked On!" I don't remember the scripture. I don't remember the content. I just remember the title and thinking to myself, that one is for me.

Even though we may not have been thrown in a dumpster like Freddie, we each have been devalued by someone close to us or some bully that was sent to distract us from our real purpose and calling in life.

People used to say in middle and high school, "You think you're pretty!" "Look at Miss America!" "Hey Miss Sweeney. You think you're Miss America!" I used to wonder, *how do they know what I think*? I wasn't thinking any of that. Maybe they did. But I was thinking I was just an average young girl going to school.

But let me tell you! You would be surprised at the number of people watching you. Baby, you're on somebody's radar and they are checking your every movement. They know more about you almost than you know about yourself.

No matter what they know about you or think they know about you, they definitely don't know what God knows about you. He is the one with the plan to prosper you and give you a future. He is the one that created you and put gifts on the inside and outside of you. God is the one that redeemed you and knows your intrinsic value. And what God has for you, it is for you. The world didn't give it, and the world can't take it away. Let them try to intimidate you. Let them talk. Talk is cheap. Their negative opinions are worthless. Their glares are impervious.

When it boils right down to it, Jesus is my only friend. And when the enemy assails in word or deed, do like the hymn says, "Take it to the LORD in prayer!"
Remember, the battle is not yours. It's the LORD's! Can I get an "Amen?" I'm preaching to myself. Yes, LORD. There is a war going on. A supernatural war. And you need to be prepared for spiritual warfare. Because these attacks and attempts to make you feel insecure are not merely flesh and blood. Ephesians 6:12 teaches, "For we wrestle not against flesh and blood, but against principalities, against the rulers of the darkness of this world, against spiritual wickedness in high places."

The Message Bible Translation

"And that about wraps it up. God is strong, and He wants you strong. So take everything the Master has set out for you, well-made weapons of the best materials. And put them to use so you will be able to stand up to everything the devil throws your way. This is no weekend war that we'll walk away from and forget about in a couple of hours. This is for keeps, a life-or-death fight to finish against the devil and all his angels."

You better take your soul security as seriously and more serious than they do homeland security. According to www.usa.gov, the Homeland Security Department's work includes customs, border, and immigration enforcement, emergency response to natural disasters, antiterrorism work and cybersecurity.

Now, put all of that in a spiritual context. We don't have time to play with it. First, secure yourself, and then handle your business and secure family and others you're assigned to minister to.

I know you may feel like you've been thrown away by the very one who was supposed to love you, provide for you, take care of you, and protect you. The God kind of relationship was just not there. You may think you're unworthy, unwanted, and unloved. That's a lie.

As one of my good friends used to say, "I don't receive that!" Pennie Harris would throw her hand up as if saying "talk to the hand" and say, "I don't receive that!"

When you find yourself in the war zone, the insecure zone, the everybody is picking on me zone, they're talking about me zone, single because I chose God's standards zone, Yes, I'm holier than thou want me to be zone, or whatever you name it zone: ______________________,
Remember the heavenly father knows how to ambush your enemy.

Go on and start shouting and praising God now. As soon as they started shouting and praising, GOD set ambushes against the men of Ammon, Moab, and Mount Seir as they were attacking Judah, and they all ended up dead. The Ammonites and Moabites mistakenly attacked those from Mount Seir and massacred them, 2 Chronicles 20:22-26 (MSG).

When you are about to make mighty movements in your life, you will see and experience opposition.
So, you want to overcome? So you want to win? DO THIS:

- Enlist in the right army
- Undergo appropriate training
- Possess properly maintained equipment
- Have ample supplies and back up
- Make sure you have a soldier's mindset
- Commit
- Show up
- Focus

INFERIORITY ISSUES

Despise not small beginnings, and be watchful of those who despise huge endings. Go on and tell the spectators and some of the participators,

1. I'm not done yet!

2. God is not finished with me yet.
3. God favors me!
4. It's 2024 and God's got more in store!
5. I'm so blessed, I can't be suppressed!
6. I look better than what I've been through!
7. But as for you, you meant evil against me; but God meant it for my good… Genesis 50:20
8. I'm blessed going in and blessed coming out.
9. God is still in control.
10. GOD is working this for my good!

Sometimes when you can overcome so much, other folks who were for you will turn on you.

"Whoever is not with Me is against Me, and whoever does not gather with me scatters," Matthew 12:30. Sometimes you really have got to watch them folks.

When folks can deal with you when you play small, but they can't stand you when level up, it's about time for a circle change. When folks bring a little league game to a big-league stadium, something has got to change. When you're in the golden zone or the end zone and your so-called team members are not even on the field, didn't come to practice, and are sitting up in the stadium watching and waiting for you to be defeated, get in the holy huddle with Jesus.

I guarantee, He already had your new team ready. Sometimes, the folks you start with will not be able to go with you all the way. One of the main reasons things start falling apart when you start overcoming is that you let the wrong folks stay when you were moving into your new season.

Dr. Traci Lynn's beginnings are inspirational. She started her fashion jewelry business with $200 after her previous business had failed. She says she started the business in the house. She remodeled her kitchen. Her supporters saw her prospering and decided they didn't want to support any more. They had a meeting on her porch. She heard them say, "All we're doing is helping her build her dream. Let's stop helping her." And they did. They left her because she was leveling up. They even said, "We're not gone make her rich."

Inferiority complex is constant feelings of inadequacy or insecurity in your daily life due to a belief that you are physically or mentally inferior to others, whether such a belief is based on a rational assessment or not. If you ever find yourself dealing with irrational, illogical, immature co-workers or team players, or family members, you might be dealing with someone with an inferiority complex. Inferiority complexes will make fake folks show their true colors.

Just because your initial plans don't pan out, don't just quit. Don't you start feeling inadequate, less than, and defeated. Get over it. You have the power to beat defeat. Set your new goal and remember what God says about you.

You may have started as a caterpillar, but the rebirth is amazing. Traci Lynn said she shut her business down for ten years. It was dormant.

God's time table is not necessarily going to line up with yours. But you will overcome. Even if you have to retract for a season. Stay in the place God leads you to, until He says this is the day I'm going to put you on display. Hold on to that verse that says, "This is the day that the Lord has made; We will rejoice and be glad in it," Psalm 118:24.

- First of all, notice what time it is....DAYTIME!
- Next, who made the day? Whew! THE LORD!
- Next, how many people are we talking about? More than one. WE!
- Next, what are we doing? REJOICING!
- Lastly, what are we being? GLAD IN IT!

Most of the saints have that verse down, can recite it, sing it, and shout it. But it's the next verses for me: "Save now, I beseech thee, O LORD: O LORD, I beseech thee, send now prosperity. Blessed be he that cometh in the name of the LORD: We have blessed you out of the house of LORD."

We are overcoming now because the LORD is saving now and sending prosperity now. This is a God thing.

Stop being bothered by somebody else being bothered by your blessings. Favor is not fair, final or fruitless.

When you are in a place of promise, walking in power, living in prosperity, you won't be the only one blessed. There will be residual blessings! Why? Because the Bible says in Psalm 68:19, "Blessed be the Lord, who daily loadeth us with benefits, even the God of our salvation." Keep reading the next two verses and see how God handles your issues and your enemies.

Get in the loading zone so you can get the benefits God has for you. And just be cognizant of the fact that as you become more confident in God, there will be those who begin to feel more inferior toward you.

Examine yourself and make sure you are not behaving in a haughty manner. Don't you become puffed up because you might meet the same people you passed going up on the way back down. As long as you remain humble under the mighty hand of God, He will exalt you in due season if you faint not.

I believe there is a due season coming for you. Due seasons are often unpredictable as to when they come and how long they last. But I want you to join me now thanking God in advance for your loading zone. Thank Him for the naysayers. Thank God for the process. Thank Him that He knows how much of that other stuff you can handle. The hurt, the pain, the misunderstanding, the envy, the jealousy, the haters.

Psalms 71:10 states, "For my haters are waiting secretly for me; and those who are watching for my soul are banded together in their evil designs." Haters are real.

1 Peter 4:12-13 says, "Beloved, think it not strange concerning the fiery trial which is to try you as though some strange thing happened unto you. But rejoice, inasmuch as ye are partakers of Christ's sufferings; that, when his glory shall be revealed, ye may be glad also with exceeding joy."

"A strong, positive self-image is the best possible preparation for success." -Joyce Brothers

CONSTRUCTION

- ✓ How you look to you matters. How you look to others matters too, sometimes, but how you look to God matters the most.
- ✓ You are never out of God's sight.
- ✓ Make your move with or without anybody with you.

DESTRUCTION

- ✓ Don't be intimidated.
- ✓ God did not make junk.
- ✓ Stop being bothered by somebody else being bothered by your blessings.
- ✓ Don't let negative words be spoken over you.
- ✓ Don't let people remain attached to you for comfort and convenience.

INSTRUCTION

- ✓ Reflect the image of God.
- ✓ God even multiplies double for your trouble.
- ✓ Don't wait until it's too late to obey God.
- ✓ Don't hesitate; it's almost equivalent to disobeying.
- ✓ When God says move on, MOVE!

Design your MIND SIGN:

I´M

PRICELESS!

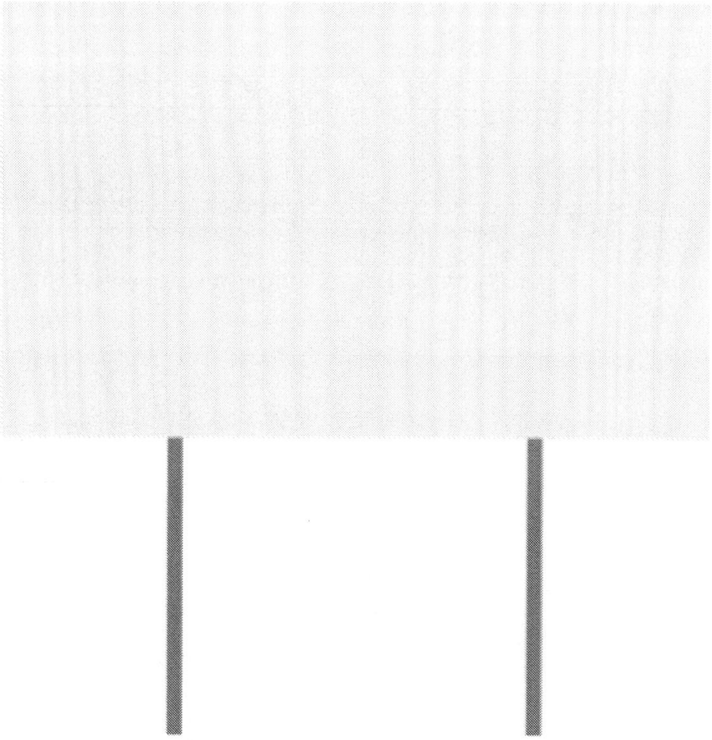

POSITIVITY PAGE Date ____________________

Issue means:

1. an important topic or problem for debate or discussion.
2. The action of supplying or distributing
3. Come, go or flow out from

How did God solve a problem for you recently? Or what dilemma do you need worked out now?

____

____

____

____

____

What has God supplied for in the way of a surprise blessing? Expect it if you haven't received it.

____

____

____

____

____

How is the light of God flowing out of you, causing you to reflect him in this dark world?

____

____

Daily Actuation Plan (DAP)

1. Pray that you hear what God says about you and live in that truth.

2. Put the whole armor of God on. What is the most meaningful piece of armor to you? Why?

3. Be alert and prepared for spiritual warfare. List one trick of the enemy you almost missed, but God

revealed it.

Chapter 7
Get Up! Get Fit!

"As one of the humans has said, active habits are strengthened by repetition but passive ones are weakened." – C. S. Lewis

High five! It's time for a mammoth move. If you want something better, do something greater. One of the biggest zones women face and get stuck in is the weight zone. We tussle with getting to and maintain that ideal weight. We talk about it. We watch videos about it. We join gyms in hopes of doing something about it. We move from diet to diet, and even pay into "the biggest loser" at work. We change for a few days, and then it's back to the old habits.

Have you ever been that way? If not, I know you know someone who is in that boat right now. They're in a fix, and they feel like they can't get fit. They will even tell you they've tried everything, and nothing worked. And you, having done the same thing, will agree. And then there you all go out for pizza, wings, and something to drink so you can commiserate about whatever happens to be going on in your lives now.

Why do we get in that cycle of depressive behavior? Because misery loves company. Even more, misery loves comfort. Your comfort zones make sure you are around the people who condone (right or wrong) what you do and the habits you have. But I will tell you like Dr. Bridget Hillard said in a sermon she preached, "Get away from people who have your problem. Get with people who have your solution. Cut the suckers loose!"

If I can get you to think about the way you think about something, perhaps you will be more mindful in making decisions and taking action to reaching those missed goals. I believe if you really want to move out of a place of mediocrity and metamorphosize into a new you, metacognition is key. True transformation is in an awareness of your own thought processes and an understanding of the patterns behind them. The term comes from the root word *meta*, which means beyond or on top of. So, make up your mind before it's too late. Go beyond your present state and get on top of all the issues that are hindering your progress.

Some of you are stuck in the place you're stuck because you are connected to the wrong folks who ascribe to the wrong thoughts. Some of you are stuck by yourself and your own decisions. Whatever the reason is for your stuckness, now is your time to get unstuck. In her book, *Get Unstuck! Be Unstoppable!*, Valorie Burton says, "The first step to getting unstuck is a simple one: Tell yourself the truth and behave based on that truth. It is easier said than done."

Find your truth in the Word of God. What does the Word say about your body? "Do you not know that your bodies are temples of the Holy Spirit, who is in you, whom you have received from God? You are not your own," – 1 Corinthians 6:19.

If you want to be better and do better, do something different. Don't settle for what has been. On almost every survey I have ever administered, the number one concern was regarding needing strength. Number two was losing weight. By reading and heeding the information and encouragement in this chapter, you're building your strength. If you want to overcome in the area of losing weight, there are some things you need to begin doing now.

FIVE FEED MOVES

F.I.V.E. = Faithfully Increase Victory Every-day!
F.E.E.D. = Focusing Exercising Eating Determination
M.O.V.E.S. = Mightily Overcoming Various Events Strategically
Never underestimate starting small. Celebrate starting! Get up early! Early to bed…early to rise makes a woman healthy, wealthy and wise. A great time to start is now. Terri Savelle Foy puts it this way, "Mind over mattress."

1. Practice the hour of power 20 minutes of prayer, 20 minutes of exercise, 20 minutes of reading.
2. Get a 21-day goal.
3. Start today. Guard your words. Say: "I am disciplined!"

Get up. Go from auto pilot to making that move. Mel Robbins suggests the Five Second Rule. Just say five, four, three, two, one. She felt if she didn't move within that five second window, her brain would talk her out of doing what she should have been doing.

High performance people have desire and fire, faith and action, focus and follow through. I pray this chapter will give you all of the above and do all it will take to surpass your fitness goals.

Let's get started. Most think going on a diet is the key, but most studies show that people revert to old habits even though they say they really want to lose weight or get fit. The root from which the word *diet* comes means "way of life." Diet basically means *discipline.* The denotative meaning of discipline is the practice of training people to obey rules or a code of behavior, using punishment to correct disobedience.

Guess what! If you are disobedient to what is suggested to you, I'm not coming for you to punish you. I won't even be around when you are buying and stashing those cookies, brownies, donuts, candy bars, sodas, potato chips, burgers, fries, pies, cakes, and other delicious treats. These devilish distractions are always around, and if not, they can easily be found. They're cheap and conveniently in your face at almost every store when it's time to check out.

People are always willing to give you what you don't need to eat. I have never heard anyone say, hears a pot of turnip greens. But I have heard people say, "Here's a box of pizza we had left over." Or, "Here's a whole box of donuts." There's often whole cakes brought to work counters and breakrooms, but I haven't seen any random fruit trays brought in to just nibble on. You need discipline to deal with the delectable distractions that desire to deter your progress.

If you really want to overcome in this area, you have got to make up your mind and make your actions follow these directions.

Give me FIVE!

Faithfully Increase Victory Every-day!

- 5 strong people in your orbit
- Up at 5am – praying, reading Bible
- Exercise at least 5 minutes per day
- 5 glasses of water per day
- 5 servings of veggies and fruit weekly
- Lose 5 pounds in 5 weeks (consult physician first)
- Last meal to eat at 5:00pm daily
- 5 healthy snacks only
- First five weeks No-Nos!
- No fast-food restaurants
- No bread
- No pasta
- No rice
- No desserts
- No drinks other than water
- No exceptions
- No excuses

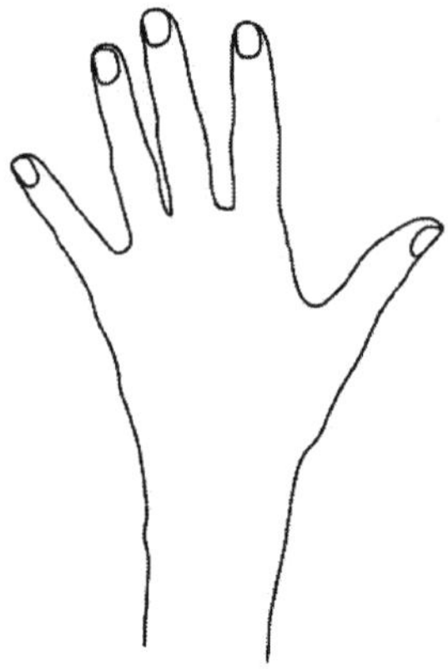

Check in with the five people in your orbit with a simple text of these 5 reports:

1. I am proud of myself because

   ____.

2. I failed to

   ____.

3. I need to

   ____.

4. I am grateful for

   ____

5. I will encourage you

   ____.

Be very careful about who you allow in your Give Me Five Orbit. They need to be as committed as you are. If they are unable to comply, it's really okay. Just move on to someone else who is. The time is out for people putting the brakes on when it comes to your progress.

The story is told of two men riding a tandem bicycle up a steep hill. After much effort, they finally made it to the top of the hill. The front rider said, "That was a tough ride." To which the second rider replied, "Sure was, and if I hadn't kept the brake on, we might have slipped backwards."

We are moving forward! Being consistent and determined will keep us moving forward and making progress.

CONSTRUCTION

- ✓ Get away from people who have your problem. Get with people who have your solution.

DESTRUCTION

- ✓ S.T.O.P. Stuff That Opposes Progress!
- ✓ Get rid of negative "I statements."
- ✓ Stop being impatient with yourself.
- ✓ Don't copy the destructive behaviors of others.

INSTRUCTION

- ✓ Don't do excuses! Do exercises!
- ✓ "Cast all your anxiety on him because he cares for you." 1 Peter 5:7
- ✓ Let your faith roar so loudly that you can't hear what doubt is saying.

Design your MIND SIGN:

POSITIVITY PAGE Date ____________________

How do you see yourself changing?

____

____

____

____

____

In what ways do you need to stop comparing yourself to others?

____

____

____

____

____

Write the names of your five in your orbit.

1. ______________________________________
2. ______________________________________
3. ______________________________________
4. ______________________________________
5. ______________________________________

Beginning date of the five-week (Get rid of five pounds challenge) ______________________

Your starting weight ______________

Week one weight ______________

Week two weight ______________

Week three weight ______________

Week four weight ______________

Week five weight ______________

Celebrate any progress. Pray over any disappointments.

Tempting foods for you:

____

Tempting drinks for you:

____

Polite/direct/final answers to offers of No-Nos

Examples of NO… "I brought my snacks today. Thank you."

"I'm enjoying water. That looks good, but no thank you."

____

____

____

____

____

"Do you not know that your body is a temple of the Holy Spirit within you, whom you have from God? You are not your own, for you were bought with a price. So glorify God in your body." 1 Corinthians 6:19-20

DAILY ACUTATION PLAN (DAP)

1. Pray for endurance.

____

____

2. Find and write a Bible verse related to people who made a move.

____

____

Part 3
Ah! Momentum

Chapter 8
Keep On Keeping On!

"Be careful for nothing; but in every thing by prayer and supplication with thanksgiving let your requests be made known unto God." (Philippians 4:6 KJV)

The best message I ever received was "KEEP ON KEEPING ON!" It was written on a greeting card my mother, Rev. Shirley Ann King Sweeney, mailed to me during my first semester of college. This powerful message arrived at a time I felt like giving up. I was disappointed and upset by the grade I made in my math class.

Of course, math was not my favorite subject. Like students, I just knew I'd never need or use the information we had to learn. Wrong. Knowledge is valuable. But more importantly, applied knowledge is valuable. I needed a reset on my mindset about math. The next semester, I passed the class. I had to keep on keeping on.

"Life be lifeing," as they say. The cycle of overcoming is like this:

- Think
- Plan
- Act
- Assess
- Modify
- Achieve
- Reflect
- Adjust
- Enhance
- Soar
- Repeat

Within that cycle of overcoming, there will always be barriers, obstacles, hurdles, blockages, aggression, opposition, road bumps, attacks, and resistance. Your dream was on the road of least resistance. However, you soon found out stuff happens.

You're flying around as that beautiful metamorphized former caterpillar now butterfly. And all of a sudden, you find yourself in a butterfly cage. Outside forces try to contain and restrain you.

While moving forward, bars keep popping up with every disappointment, disadvantage, disagreement, difficulty, delay, and defeat. If you're not careful, you'll be encaged, contained and confined.

Don't let that happen! Do whatever it takes and release and unleash all of the potential power that you possess.

THE TURNING POINT

Every cage has an opening. There is a way of escape. It's up to you to find it.

Olympia Ann LePoint went from failing to becoming a rocket scientist. Her example of resilience and sticktoitness is amazing. She coined the term *Triabrain* and created the Trianbrain Theory of Relativity in her self-help book, *Answers Unleashed: The Science of Unleashing Your Brains' Power* in 2018. She is an amazing example of not allowing personal experiences like poverty, gang violence, and sexual abuse to stop the purpose God put in her.

Trianbrain Theory of Relativity is a method to explain how she rewired her brain to overcome painful memories and succeed. Don't ever get so caught up in the cage that you forget the call. You may not be clear on all that God has called you for, but trust and believe you do have purpose.

Olympia was born in Los Angeles, California and was raised by a single mother in a poverty-stricken area. After a field trip to the Jet Propulsion Laboratory in Pasadena at the age of six, she decided to become a rocket scientist. At the age of 10, she was stabbed in the face by a gang member, which led to her transfer to a gifted magnet school where she began to fail math before a teacher helped turn around her grades.

Always know there is a way out, over, or through whatever you are dealing with. It does not mean that you won't have to go through anything. It doesn't mean there won't be dark days and sleepless nights. Empty pockets. Closed doors. High mountains. Low valley. Raging storms. Back stabs. Phony, fake, two-faced frienemies. Sickness. Death. Problems. Disasters. You name it. You may face and have to endure all of that early on in life or within a short period of time.

After graduating from high school at age sixteen, Olympia enrolled at California State University. There she survived the January 17, 1994, Northridge earthquake which destroyed the university campus, injuring 8,700, and killing one of her classmates among 56 others. She graduated in the top five of a class of 6,500. Talk about momentum. She landed a job at the Boeing Company as a mathematician at the age of 21. She was a professional rocket scientist for NASA programs.

View those difficult times as preparation for elevation. Your obstacles open opportunities. Your struggles produce your strength.

Olympia LePoint turned her pain into purpose and unleashed a wealth of power that has inspired many others. "No matter what the circumstances, you have the ability to find your way out and find success for yourself."
-Olympia LePoint

CONSTRUCTION

- ✓ Once you become fearless, life becomes limitless.
- ✓ Being enabled by a well-able God makes all things possible.
- ✓ Don't get so caught up in the cage that you forget the call.

DESTRUCTION

- ✓ Outside forces seek to contain and restrain you.

INSTRUCTION

- ✓ Be stronger than your strongest excuse.
- ✓ Small deeds done are better than great deeds planned. – Peter Marshall

Design your MIND SIGN:

Momma said:

Keep On Keeping On!

POSITIVITY PAGE Date ____________________

Write about a time when you felt like you were in a cage and kept from moving forward.

____

____

____

____

____

What is something you are afraid to try because you think you will fail at it.

____

____

____

____

____

List sources of help that can be called upon to help you reach our goals.

____

____

____

DAILY ACTUATION PLAN (DAP)

1. Write a prayer that you will be aware of the inspiration around you.

2. Reflect on how God can use your setbacks to be a set up for a breakthrough.

3. Select one person that you will encourage with a gift (a book, a card, a dinner, or a call).

Name

____

____

Deed

____

____

Chapter 9
Momentum Blockers/ Momentum Stockers

"When you want to succeed as bad as you want to breathe, then you'll be successful." -ET

Do you know you can have momentum blockers even before you get started? At around the age of twelve, Eric Thomas, now E.T., world renowned motivational speaker and preacher, had a question for his mom. He asked, "Is my dad my real dad?" The answer was no. E.T. said when he was homeless and when he dropped out of school it was because he thought his mother had him by accident. He withdrew.

He hit a momentum blocker. He changed and started hanging out with the thugs, doing poorly in school, disrespecting authority. When his behavior and defiance became so bad, he walked out of his home and became homeless. He later got his GED.

In college, he was inspired by a group called WSB – Willing Succeeding and Black. They were positive African American men talking about positive things. When the scheduled speaker for one of their events did not show up, Eric had to speak. The response was overwhelming. At nineteen, he knew he had a gift in speaking. He is not afraid to talk about his failures or his fears. He is the epitome of his book, *Average Skill, Phenomenal Will.* He believes in grinding. If you are willing to grind, you can have success. Be inspired by him.

Maybe what you thought would work didn't work or isn't working. Start over. What better time to start over than now. Today just may be the day that success comes your way. Choose not to give up, but to wake up. Don't sleep walk through life unable to see possibilities of a better life.

What is it going to take for you to wake up and recognize what's blocking you? For ET, it was a preacher who reached out to him. For some, a teacher, a relative, or even a stranger can make the difference.

Wherever you get your inspiration and your push from, take it, use it, and get to moving. Once you start your Aha Movement, keep it going.

If the Aha Movement is gaining new knowledge or understanding it in a new way, then Ah Momentum is doing something with that knowledge and understanding.

How many notepads, packets, handouts, and t-shirts do you have to have before you start putting into action what you were taught?

*** MOMENTUM BLOCKER:** Inaction – all mouth and no action.

Change conference was the very first conference I asked my husband if I could plan at our church. He gave permission. I was too excited. But what got me was the question my husband raised next and would often ask after I went to speak at other conferences. "Did they change?" He would say, "I wonder how many of them really changed." And of course, before I got really delivered of having something to say when feeling some kind of way, I would retort, "I wonder how many people really changed when you preached last Sunday." He would just give me a look. But now I'm delivered…from that. And I too want to know if with all the preaching and teaching, worshiping, counseling, modeling, and mentoring going on, is anybody going beyond the aha moment and reaching the Aha Movement and Ah! Momentum? That's what's needed.

Don't just absorb the information, the knowledge, the inspiration, the insight; apply it.

* **MOMENTUM STOCKER:** Application – use the knowledge you gain.

* **MOMENTUM BLOCKER:** Self-doubt: Having desire, but no fire

This book. I have talked about it. I've taken copious notes. I've watched inspirational videos. I've interviewed numerous people. I've conducted workshops. I've gathered data from surveys. I've attended conferences. But, I still had self-doubt. I had a great mindset and even a reset mindset. I had Aha Movement. I started writing and wrote a lot. But this momentum blocker called self-doubt trapped me in a cage that I thought I couldn't get out of. It wasn't until I realized that the cage was locked from within and that I had the key that I got out. Hallelujah! Thank You, Jesus! You can be your own key, too. You are your own keysmith.

*** MOMENTUM STOCKER:** Self-drive: I Know I Can Attitude

Excellence in Academics (EIA) was an afterschool program I started during my second year of teaching in middle school. I had a strong desire to make sure that students who were at risk, average, overlooked, undervalued, mistreated, or struggling had a place to study and receive professional tutoring at no cost to their parents. I got permission from my principal, Mr. Jeff Stevens, to hold the sessions twice a week. It went so well that he found funding for snacks, for paying the teachers who tutored, buses to take the participants home, and celebrator events. I was driven to do the program with no funding. Because of that can-do-attitude and drive, momentum picked up and kept going. That was the year I was voted Teacher of the Year. I was just doing what I knew God put in my heart.

Where there is a will, there is a way. Your deficiency is no match for God's sufficiency.

*** MOMENTUM BLOCKER:** Low standards – not doing your best

"A Carpenter's House" by Azailia

A highly skilled carpenter who had grown old was ready to retire. He told his employer contractor of his plans to leave the house building business and live a more leisurely life with his family. He would miss the paycheck, but he needed to retire.

The employer was sorry to see his good worker go and asked if he would build just one more house as a personal favor. The carpenter agreed to this proposal, but made sure that this would be his last project. Being in a mood to retire, the carpenter was not paying much attention to building the house. His heart was not in his work. He resorted to poor workmanship and used inferior materials. It was an unfortunate way to end his career.

When the job was done, the carpenter called his employer and showed him the house. The employer handed over some papers and the front door key to the carpenter and said, "This is your house, my gift to you."

The carpenter was in a shock! What a shame! If he had only known that he was building his own house, he would have made it better than any other house that he ever built!

Everything we do, we do unto ourselves before it goes out to the world. Be sure to put love into each of your actions.

*** MOMENTUM STOCKER:** High Standards – always do your best not just for yourself

Dr. Ida Scudder founded the Christian Medical College and Hospital in Vellore, India. As reported in an article from Vellore CMC Foundation, she decided to carry on the work of a medical missionary and raised money to build a hospital. The tiny clinic she started is now CMC Vellore- one of India's most prestigious private hospitals and medical institutions. Today, CMC cares for over two million patients and trains one thousand doctors, nurses and other medical professionals each year.

"You will not only be curing diseases but will also be battling with epidemics, plagues and pestilences and preventing them. Face trials with a smile, with head erect and a calm exterior. If you are fighting for the right and for a true principle, be calm and sure and keep on until you win." – Dr. Ida S. Scudder

*** MOMENTUM BLOCKER:** Impaired vision- unclear, unfocused, cataract covered, diseased

One of the most telling surveys I have done to date is the one in which I asked the questions, "What are the best things you see about yourself?" "What are the worst things you see in yourself?" The most shocking aspect about the survey was not the answers to those questions but the fact that the list for the worst thing was ten times longer than the best thing. This tells me there are problems. Mostly vision problems. Responders were so caught up with the cloud of negative things that they could not see their own God-given beauty, skills, calling, and anointing.

*** MOMENTUM STOCKER:** Good Why-sight (eyesight)

My daughter, Jessica, is a registered nurse (MSN, BSN, RN) who wanted eyeglasses for years. We knew she didn't need them. She knew she didn't really need them. She just wanted them. She even went to the optometrist for an eye exam. Initially, she did not need them. However, after working as a charge nurse and a clinical instructor, she finally got her wishes – a prescription for glasses to improve her eyesight.

I'm proud of Jessica for her work in the medical field, but I'm even more proud of the fact that she has always had excellent "why-sight" even from a young age. Knowing your *why* is an automatic momentum stocker. When you lead, work, and serve with heart, momentum is a given.

"Why-sight" allows you not only to see what's immediately in front of you, but what's on down the road. Jessica earned her master's degree because of "why-sight." I'll keep watching to see what else she'll accomplish. Let her be inspiration to you as you begin building momentum.

Fill in the blanks:

* MOMENTUM BLOCKER: Deficiency

____

____

____

____

* MOMENTUM STOCKER: Efficiency

____

____

____

____

"Ah! Momentum is both personal and private, but the results are visible and public." ~ah!

CONSTRUCTION

- ✓ If you can get it, can you keep it?
- ✓ Momentum is just strength gained by motion.
- ✓ Be your own keysmith.

DESTRUCTION

- ✓ You can have average skill, but develop phenomenal will. -ET
- ✓ "Your deficiency is not match for God's sufficiency." ~ah!

INSTRUCTION

- ✓ Don't allow anyone to sow weeds in the garden of your mind.

Design your MIND SIGN:

LOCKED IN TO WIN!

POSITIVITY PAGE Date ____________________

What classes or degrees or certifications are you looking forward to attaining?

____

____

____

____

____

What is your WHY? Not just why are you in the wrong zone, but why will you not stop until you get to your COMEFORTH ZONE?

____

____

____

____

____

What has blocked your momentum?

____

____

____

____

____

Which formula should you use?

Formula 1:

Made-up mind − Distractions + Focused Actions **X** Daily

Good Habits = Positive Momentum

Formula 2:

Indecision + Distractions − Focused Actions **X** Daily

BadvHabits = Negative Momentum

Chapter 10
Beat Defeat

"The difficulties and struggles of today are but the price we must pay for the accomplishments and victories of tomorrow." – William J. H. Boetcker

I believe you can beat defeat now.

I believe you know how to get over it, and you will get over it!!! IT…whatever IT is!

IT:

Initial thoughts

Ignorant thinking

Independent tasks

Irrational targets

Irresponsible teaching

Idiot train

Individual trials

Increasing trouble

Intense trauma

"What you don't want is all words and no work, all talk and no tasks, all decisions and no deliverables." ~ah!

DECISIONS! DECISIONS! DECISIONS!

It reminds me of the story of the three frogs. There were three frogs who sat on a log. One decided and declared I'm jumping off. How many frogs were left on the log?

Most would say, TWO. But in life, the answer is often THREE. Just because the one frog decided to jump off the log and even said he was jumping off the log did not mean he jumped off the log.

Is there a gap between what you decide you're going to do, say you're going to do, and what you actually do?

DO THE WORK

It's going to take work for you to get out of the wrong zones and into the COMEFORTH ZONES. And I have learned over the years, no one can do the work for you. The hours are long. The pay may not seem adequate. You may feel unappreciated, misunderstood, and overlooked. But keep working on yourself.

Happy New YOU!

Bette Nesmith was working at a bank in Dallas when she noticed a problem that piqued her interest. Was there a more efficient way to correct errors she made on her typewriter? You know this is back in the day. Bette had some art experience and knew artist could just paint over their mistakes. So, she concocted a fluid to use to paint over her errors. Then all the secretaries in the building wanted what she called "MistakeOut."

She attempted to sell the product idea to marketing agencies and various companies (including IBM), but they turned her down. However, secretaries continued to like her product. So, Bette's kitchen became her first manufacturing facility. The tiny bottles were earning $3.5 million annually. Finally, the Gillette Company bought it for $47.5 million dollars.

Sometimes your mission will find you in the middle of a mess. Sometimes your purpose will find you in the middle of a problem. If it's a problem for you, it just might be a problem for somebody else. That's how your personal victory can be a victory for the larger community and maybe even for the world. So don't allow defeat to be the end all; let it be the beginning of victory.

Each day is another opportunity to whiteout or MistakeOut what didn't go well the day before. Listen, don't wait until December 31st, to take the opportunity to do a mindset reset. Do it today.

Every day can be NEW YOU DAY! One list of New Year's resolutions for 2024 included:

1. Improve fitness
2. Improve finances
3. Improve mental health
4. Weight loss
5. Make more time for loved ones
6. Smoking cessation
7. Learn a new skill
8. Make time for hobbies
9. Improve diet
10. Improve work-life balance
11. Travel more
12. Meditate regularly

13. Drink less alcohol
14. Perform better at work

Decide which ones you will incorporate in your Happy New You Solutions.

CONSTRUCTION

- ✓ What you don't want is all words and no work, all talk and no tasks, all decisions, and no deliverables. ~ah!
- ✓ Don't allow anyone to sow weeds in the garden of your mind.
- ✓ You can either be the one defeated or the one defeating. ~ah!
- ✓ Outstanding people have one thing in common: an absolute sense of mission. -Zig Ziglar

DESTRUCTION

- ✓ Don't let age, lack of education, finances, or naysayers make you settle for the old you.
- ✓ Don't let emotions exclusion, or racism cause you to live in yesteryear.
- ✓ Don't get defeated by doubt before you get started.

INSTRUCTION

- ✓ Make sure you check your "why-sight" regularly.
- ✓ Pray without ceasing.
- ✓ Say bye to the lies.

POSITIVITY PAGE Date ____________________

What will you include on your NEW YOU RESOLUTION LIST?

1. ____
2. ____
3. ____
4. ____
5. ____
6. ____
7. ____
8. ____
9. ____
10. ____

Write out plans, strategies, and steps to get there:

____

____

____

____

____

____

____

DAILY ACTUATION PLAN (DAP)

Move from thought to decision to plans to actions.

1. Spend time in prayer. Use a prayer journal.
2. Listen to God.
3. Tell God what you want Him to know, kelp you with, do for you fix or handle.
4. Listen to God and write what He says for you to do.
5. Write down one decision you have made to start on your New YOU.

   ____

   ____

6. Set a reasonable amount of time to get that accomplished. Put a date on it. ________________
7. Make one contact outside your comfort zone that will lead to your success.
8. Journal what failures or successes you experienced regarding number 5.
9. What resources do you think you need?

   ____

10. Share your plan with your orbit. Listen and respond to their advice and/or questions.

"Personal improvement is inevitable if we don't mistake correction for dislike or conviction for disdain. Any comeuppance received has more to do with self than others. Introspection is necessary." ~ah!

Acknowledgments

To God be the Glory for the great things He has done. I will sing His praise forever. I thank Him for putting many people in my life who have encouraged me along my writing journey. I thank LeAnn Ross for introducing me to Linda Gilden. It was the Christian Writers Conference that kept me encouraged as a writer.

I can't thank Ginelle Barry enough for generously blessing me with a new laptop when my old one crashed. May God bless you for blessing one of His daughters, having just met me a couple hours before going to Best Buy.

I appreciate you, Mary Thomas, for encouraging me with The Audrey V. Hailstock COMEFORTH ZONE Fund at the Spartanburg County Foundation.

Special prayer sisters and their husbands are amazing. Thank you, Dr. Greg and Dr. Velinda Simmons. Thank you, Apostle Ryan and Pastor Erika McJimpsey.

Thank you for encouraging me to write the book and get over fear, Mary Pitts.

Great thanks and love for every person who came to the COMEFORTH ZONE. Your attendance, insight, questions, and willingness to learn mean everything to me. I have record of how you have changed and grown. I say there is more in store.

Rebecca Pearl, thank you for your unwavering faith, beautiful disposition, and connection.

Emmanuella Rodenberg, thank you for coaching me and telling me to put a date on having my book published.

Thank you for the front cover design, La J'ai Reed.

Thank you, Jessica Hailstock, my phenomenal daughter, for hyping me up.

About the Author

Audrey Hailstock is a playwright, author, motivational and inspirational speaker, gospel preacher, ordained minister, praise and worship leader, Sunday School and Bible study teacher, and a former middle school English and drama teacher. She is a graduate of Erskine College. She has served as president of Spartanburg Toastmasters Speaking Out at the Y, secretary of the SC Congress of Christian Education, lecturer in the Ministers' Wives Division of the National Congress of Christian Education. She is the president of the Spartanburg County Alliance of Ministers' Wives and Ministers' Widows spoken and preached in the Southeast Regional and the International Association of Ministers' Wives and Minsters' Widows.

Audrey has established The Audrey V. Hailstock COMEFORTH Zone Fund 2142 which provides support for women who step out of their comfort zones into a place of empowerment. She enjoys preaching, writing, singing, sewing, and exercising. She is married to Dr. James L. Hailstock, and they have two outstanding children – Alex and Jessica. Audrey is an atmosphere, trajectory, and destiny changer!

Hadasssah's
Crown Publishing, LLC

Made in the USA
Columbia, SC
02 June 2025

58797488R00098